thank you. yes, you, the o~

to the ones who don't

to the ones looking to squ

last drop of light. to the one~ ~till busy

chasing adventures. to the ones who are

reckless. to the ones who seek the truth

and not opinion. to all of my loved ones,

whom without, i would not be here today.

to my muse and hidden secret.

this is for you.

"one day, when i look back at my life and i'm sitting

in my chair, staring out towards who i used to be,

i want to be able to say, you know what, i did it.

i made it and exceeded my own expectations."

-z.k.d

A Journal From The Sea

by Zachry K. Douglas

it starts behind the eyes and a fire

burns inside my throat. i'm begging

it to stop. tears, why do you fall so

fast? heart, why can't you sleep?

quiet the ache inside of me please.

i turn over, the ceiling fan can't seem

to make enough noise to silence the

concert in my chest.

i tell myself it will be okay.
i tell myself it will be okay.

someday.

i will never need a kingdom to

be a king. conquer what lives

inside your walls and you'll have

all the power one will ever need.

i am a student being taught by
the pile of stars that never had
a chance.

they tell me, "the fallen find
peace in things others never
see."

she stopped looking for love when she
finally found it within herself. she is her
own savior. a power created from all the
lies and bullshit she had once put up
with.

now, instead of giving all her time away,
she's taking it all back with a laugh and
a middle finger to the world.

i need to know your skin. i need to know how it feels when i take you to your place where you grab the sheets, while i get a handful of your hair and pull back to see if your lips taste like the moans coming from them.

i need to know your skin and how it feels to be naked with you.

now, please.

what it all comes down to is,
knowing when to hold them
tighter and telling them how
much they truly mean to you
every goddamn chance you get.

love is knowing without the
other, your soul would literally
break in half.

and we wonder why the moon
comes in phases.

she didn't do everything the right way.
it was not her code. she read her books
and drank her wine alone most of the
time. but it was during those quiet
moments of solitude, she mapped out
how to conquer the universe, one glass
at a time and one chapter at a time.
her mind was her weapon and it has
killed many of men who thought she
was just another pretty face. they said
she was wasting her life, but those who
thought that never knew she was holding
onto the idea of a love made just for her.
and so she continued to smile every
chance she got.

she said to herself,

"the only people squandering
time, are the ones worried about
not having enough."

when eyes cease to fall at night.

when lips begin to read the soul.

when hearts repeat each burning

beat of love. when hands turn into a

religion your body needs, that's when

you let go of what you've known and

accept what you have always deserved.

i don't just want to take in life with you.
i want to go to dinner with you and talk
about random things that make us laugh.
i want to carry you to bed when you've
had a long day and lay with you while
playing with your hair. i want to shower
with you, because there's nothing more
intimate than cleansing the soul together.
i want to be in the kitchen with you,
because you love to cook and i want to do
and try the things you love. it's important
to me that you are cared for when you
don't ask for it. it's in these moments i
want to live with you while having no
rules as to how to love. it's what makes us
who we are. these are the things i need
while needing you in my life always.

my sky is empty without you.

she does something otherworldly.

she wakes up and makes me forget

how much pain lives inside of me.

he holds her as if it
was his last breath.

fighting taught him
how to lose a battle.

love taught him how
to win a war.

she never forgot where she came from.
a place that holds people responsible for
what they do and don't do. it's the inner
strength she has that makes everyone
around her stronger. she's a barefoot
princess who's known to walk through
fire when pushed beyond her limits.
she has endured a life only a few could
have survived and still enjoys the rainy
days. there's a peace that lives within her
eyes and exudes the most beautiful kind
of confidence. she is sexy, but not for the
clothes she wears or the makeup on her
face.

she's all natural down to her core and
when she loves, she always gives a little
more.

in the naked of the light,
her body brings me to my
knees. she knows what she
wants, so i confess to her the
sins i am going to commit by
whispering them to her as i tie
each one of her hands to the bed
posts.

covering up her eyes, i begin.

she has this innate ability

to be herself in a world that

constantly screams at her to

change.

she's original like that.

she is a sunday morning wrapped in
blankets, because she is in love with
her bed, but she is the furthest thing
from lazy. she is driven and focused
on making the best out of every day
she is given. her room is her safe haven
and where most of her best ideas are
turned into a playbook for an undefeated
spirit.

the kind that likes to smile as she battles
those believing she is anything but
extraordinary.

she's always two moves ahead, before you
realize you've already lost.

she has a closest full of dreams and each
outfit is her own personal style. but her
favorite things to wear are her dancing
shoes and a dress that hugs her body like
a warming pair of hands. wherever this
wild child ventures to, she's going to
make it a night to remember.

one shot and she's letting her down.
two shots and she's talking to new
friends. three shots and she's her own
party. she enjoys the company of a good
conversation and sounds of laughter
around her. you could say she's different,
but that's the way she likes it.

she asked me with anxiety in her voice,
"will you love me even on my bad days?"

it took all i had to stand as tall
as the man i am, without falling
anymore for the beauty that was
in front of me,

"yes, sweetheart, i will love you even on
your bad days. for there was a time when
we didn't have any days to speak of.
now that we have had them, i want more
for the rest of my life. i need our days.
you are the breath i take in."

she doesn't need to be saved.

just the right type of loving

that makes her feel safe.

even when she stands alone in her own
beliefs, a crowd always seems to gather
when she speaks.

there's something absolutely beautiful
about a woman who is not afraid to say
what's on her mind.

she's wildly weird in
a world stuffed full of
ordinary. the only time
she cries is when she's
alone with her own heart.
at night before she sleeps,

she finds peace in the warming
words she reads. she dances to
the sounds others cannot hear.

she might be a little crazy, but not
being herself, life for this snowflake
would be incredibly boring.

without a question in her voice, she told
me, "i do not want promises, just days
and nights like these." i couldn't help but
put my arms around her and make sure
she felt the love i have for her in me.
heart to heart, i said, "i will never give you
empty promises. i will give you these days
and nights until there is no more of me to
give. you will never hurt alone. you will
never have to hide from your fears,
because i will be fighting them with you.
your head will always sleep on our stars
and i will be lying next to you, falling in
love with a life together which will outlast
every single constellation we call home."
pulling her in tighter, i told her, "at times,
this place will take away your breath and
make you feel helpless without air to fill
your lungs. together, we will never run
out of love to breathe. we both know it
won't be easy, but to one day die beside
you and live another life with you will be
the highest honor for me. fall into me and
rest your bones, sweet woman. i have you
now and forever."

she is a delicate flower in the month
of may, but still has thorns for those
expecting an easy fight.

she'll leave you and move on if you're
unworthy of a love like hers.

she doesn't ask for much. all she wants
is someone to make her feel warm during
the cold nights and soothe the ache in her
heart.

an ache created by a trust that was
broken.

it was in the sky where she found pieces
of those who had left her. each sunset
and sunrise brought out the very best
in this unbreakable woman. she knew
whatever happened, she would be able
to outlast the pain and heartache from
her past, because of what was above her.

she took her time and took in all the
colors the ones had painted for her.
though at times it brings tears to her
eyes, the sight of what she sees allows
love to sprinkle throughout her world.

she doesn't need
to be cool to fit in.

she's her own
school of misfits.

i stuck my head outside the window

of the moon and screamed into the

universe, "i will find you in this life

and love you endlessly in the home

of eternity."

it's in the way she carries herself.
as if she has always known she was
born with wings. a gentle set of lungs
breathes in love and forms a melody
sung by the stars in her soul.

she is the only thing my eyes have
ever known. i used to wonder why
they looked to the moon so often...

but now i know.

i hope you find someone who loves you.
someone who loves you without having
to say a word. someone who can hold you
without using their arms. someone who
knows how to be there for you when you
find yourself unable to get up off the floor.
someone who gets you and understands
the qualities that others may have found
odd or annoying. someone who doesn't
mind getting up a little before you do,
just to make sure the water is warm and
there's a towel beside the shower.

someone who will take their time to leave
a note or a simple reminder on the fridge
that explains how today is better because
of you. someone who gets home and isn't
too tired to hug you with all the energy
that is left in them and kisses you as if the
sky was on fire. someone who needs to
know where you go when the world gets
too big for you so they can meet you
there.

i hope you find someone who
loves you and i hope they are
there to love you when the
lights go out.

please do not look at the one story home
with twelve windows and think nothing
magical ever happened in it because it's
thirty years old and has stains on the
outside. even if bad things did happen
underneath that roof made from black
clouds, it's still standing. sleepless nights
and screams were heard throughout the
walls, and if you go there i'm sure you can
still hear the echoes of a troubling
childhood; the laughs, the cries,
the sneaking out of the window at night,
the lonely bedroom where parents used
to sleep, a backyard where countless
basketball games were played and life
decisions were made. a swimming pool
that had enough water splashed out of it
that it could fill the oceans again.

all is still there and all of me used to live
there. a mother still lives the now and
she sits in her chair and smokes cigarettes,
staring out into the backyard, picturing
her boys still playing. a man sits at his
desk and types this for others to read,
letting them know they are not alone.
a man as old as that house with two
windows. please do not think nothing
magical ever happened in the things you
cannot see inside of. most of the time,
all you need is a glimpse of hope to build
a dream.

i am still building my own, and i am still
standing.

she has a way with words,
even when she doesn't speak.
an uncommon type some would
say.

one that gets misunderstood for
standing up when others are walking
on their knees. she has her walls and
boundaries, but that's because she
knows what she wants.

she's life all wrapped up in elegance,
with a touch of attitude. just enough
to make the night last a little longer.

she has dreams just like any other
self-searching woman.

it starts in the morning when the
mirror tells her,

"this is your day. whatever reflection
others try and show you, never believe
a talking head who has no soul."

she.
she is not mine.
but she is the smile on my face and the
chills i feel when the night showcases the
moon.
she.
she is not mine.
but maybe one day she could be.
she is the reason why constellations were
given names.

she owns all that i know i am.

all of her life, she had heard,
"just survive a little longer.
it gets better."

when surviving became something she
couldn't stand anymore, she began to
fight like hell and take back what was
rightfully hers; a life. a smile. a heart.
a soul. a mind. all that makes a human
more than just a body.

she became selfish with all of it.
and you know what, she wears them all
now like the sky wears the stars at night.
when knowing what you want is not what
you need anymore, surviving will never
be enough.

it's her battle cry.

just know there will be times when i'll
need you and i'll be a fucking mess.
when none of my words will make sense
and my tears interrupt the silence
in-between a much needed breath.
just know there will be moments when
i cannot stand on my own, because the
weight of my anger and sadness will pull
me down. there will be days when i'll
need someone to talk to, because talking
to myself isn't enough. completely losing
it and breaking down in front of the ones
you love is what at times makes it worse,
as you try and hold it in to keep people
from thinking you are weak. but trust me,
it's okay. it's human and sometimes being
a human sucks. i cannot tell you how
many of those times, moments, or days
there will be, but i can promise you this,
everything is better when you're standing
next to me.

life has always tried to keep her down.
it's been that way ever since she started
becoming more of who she was born to
be. even with the comments she hears,
the stares she gets, and the universe
constantly throwing darkness around her,
the resiliency to be herself creates the
stars she needs during the rough times.
she loves a good challenge and is always
capable of exceeding expectations. to be
brave and courageous even under scrutiny
for being different is a testament of just
how big her heart actually is.

and to be honest, she doesn't give a damn
about acceptance from those unwilling to
see past their own insecurities.

she has faith, but not in certain people.
too many times she has been screwed
over, which left a permanent reminder
for future relationships. all she ever
wanted was a castle made from love.
not a pile of ruins created by disguised
truth.

it's not that she has given up.
she simply gave up on those
who only saw themselves
when they looked at her.

she gets tired from all the people asking

things of her. she's a helpful human and

is considerate of others, but there comes

a time when her eyes close and all is right

again with the world. even though she

rises with the moon, she still yearns for a

night off. she's a powerful entity and

knows how to shine when the time is

needed. she'll learn how not to give away

all of her energy. she's too brilliant not to.

for even angels need their rest.

these are the things you need to know
about me, darling. i will make sure i am
the first one up to care for you, so you
don't have to lay there alone.

i will bring you food when your eyes
haven't fully opened yet, so you can
rest in our bed a little longer. i will
not leave you by yourself, even when
you tell me you don't want to talk to
me.

i will be right there to make sure you
know i won't leave when i know you
need me. when days come where we
are not together and miles apart,

please understand this about me,
you will always sleep in my heart.
you are my sweet love and the kiss
goodnight the moon gives to the
stars.

for the first time in her
life, she has given herself
permission to unpack her
wings. she's setting off on
a new adventure. one that
will test her soul, but deep
down she knows nothing
fun ever comes from doing
just the ordinary. she will fly
without any direction. it's all
about feeling this time.
she was always destined for
greater things, even if it took
her a while to come to terms
with doing better than what
she accepted. now it's her
mantra. she is stronger now
than she was and more focused
on her needs. we all have choices
and she finally gave herself one.

turns out, it was the only one she
ever needed.

she walks a little slower these days,
but her steps are still as meaningful
as the first ones she ever took.
her head doesn't look up to the sky
as much, but she still looks forward as
often as she can.

her body has become weak and has lost
some of the weight she tried to put on to
overcome the bones that were showing.
she still laughs and tells stories of when
she was younger. the days when she wore
her hair past her shoulders, or curled if
the event called for it. now she wears a
pink bandana around her head. not for
a fashion statement, but for a peace of
mind. she has grit and moxie. the kind
you find in fighters.
she tells me,

"one day soon, i will wear flowers in my
hair again."

she looked at me with all her being and held my eyes as if she had known this moment was coming, "you've made me laugh the hardest under the stars." without being able to say a word at first, i brought my finger to my heart and then pointed up above our heads. with a sentence starting to form, like a thousand rivers being born, i held her eyes next, "when a soul is attached to the idea that love is made from a promise kept within the stars inside of us, only then can it understand just how sacred sharing the same sky really is."

you don't want to be with a guy like me.
i will tell you how beautiful you are,
even after the millionth time you tell
me that you are not. i will take you to the
ocean, not to look at it, but to look at you
dance within its precious waves. i will not
be able to give you all of the finer things
others may be able to give. all i can offer
you is my heart for now. i will take you to
my parent's house. not for them to judge
you, but for them to see what love
actually looks like in person.

i do not have the best life others say they
have. i just have myself and these words
that have been written for you ever since
i started breathing. i'm not naive and
i see the life out in front of me, but forgive
me if i do not wish to see love the way
they make it out to be. you don't want to
be with a guy like me. i am everything
they tell you is wrong with society.
but if that means loving more than most,
giving my all to a cause i feel is worthy,
in love with the universe, and the thrill of
chasing every single breath of yours,
then maybe i am not the guy you want to
be with.

her family is her circle. it is the lifeblood
of all the things that make her who she
is.

they get crazy at times and let the world
know they weren't created just to go
through the motions. they laugh harder
than most and use profanity in their
jokes.

they are what some would call a wild crew.
together, they have been taking down the
universe, star by star, ever since they
knew how to smile back at those who
didn't understand their
humor.

you are the reason my blood is finally

warm again. you are the dancing flames

around my burning sun. a kind of love

time cannot steal away.

it can only watch and take notes knowing

it's in the presence of two worlds existing

as one.

the truth is, when i tell myself i want to
be alone, i want nothing else than to be
with you. because a life without you,
my best friend, would be equivalent to
the sun never rising again to kiss the
moon. i swear i hear the walls talking
about past conversations we've had
from the nights before. when time
would ricochet off the sky and come
back as feelings we couldn't find.
maybe we can discover a common place
where our love can finally come up for air
and breathe in the life we want to have.
from the time we began our friendship
and what it has grown into today, i hear
more and more people tell me, "it's funny
what happens in a year and who is brave
enough to stay." i laugh with them and
agree. it's amazing what

happens when you allow vulnerability to take over in such a way, your life becomes the very thing you never want to clothe again. my words, my soul, my heart, all of me is finally able to see the real qualities others had tried to keep from my sight. was i that bad? was i a monster hiding under my own bed? no, i was merely a ghost trapped in his own darkness who was afraid of the light. now i know who i am, because of the way you so graciously held me when others were so quick to let me fall on my own. the balance of life and love comes to those who wish to rise and fall together.

it's what you and i have learned together.

she speaks love into all the things that
never knew of it before. her mind is her
battlefield, but she is a warrior and knows
what it takes to defeat anything or anyone
who gets in her way. she doesn't get
caught up in the madness around her.
she is the madness. if you think she is
scared of a few more scars, i hope you are
ready for the fight of your life. she is more
than just a woman of reason. she is the
reason why the sky carries the stars in
such a meaningful way. whether or not
you believe in things like that, she will
always be a colorful season of change.
doing things because she can,
when everyone else is giving up
and walking away.

in her life, she hasn't had that many
people she could count on.

everyone either let her down, or would
eventually run out of lies to tell her.

it was a shame because she wanted so
badly to believe in something more than
her own words. at least they were the
honest truth.

no matter how horrible her day was,
or how long she had to work, her own
motivation carried her throughout each
second of her life.

it's a tiresome act and walking on a wire
becomes a deathly adventure if you
happen to hold onto too much of what
needs letting go. she has a lot going for
her and she knows it.

at times though, it helps when you can
take a deep breath and remember what
keeps you moving forward.

she does it often, while balancing on the
stars.

she has eyes that see through the tears
she cries and a heart that won't allow
her to fail. she is headstrong when it
comes to trying to solve the equations
of life and love. she's a walking fire
starter who craves the open water and
the feel of sunshine on her naked skin.
but she is just as content with the rolling
clouds and heavy rains as long as she is
wearing her socks and has a few blankets
to wrap up with. she enjoys the alone time.
for her, she'd rather spend it by herself
than giving it to someone who takes more
than just the covers when they leave.
some would call her a shot of whiskey
after last call, but she is the glass of wine
yet to be poured. it's all about savoring
the first breath of the moon when it
comes to living her life.

in life, we all have those
times when family completes
all the needs we long for;
a simple laugh.
a simple joke.
a simple hug.

all of which brings us back to where we
belong. and sometimes it takes us back to
when the world sang alongside our hearts,
as we found the melody needed in order
to start again.

i guess i could lie and tell you i am
different. that i don't cry and let my
emotions get the best of me. so instead,
i'll be honest with you. there are times
when i could be stronger and not fold
over with the moon at night. i have
feelings rush over me of which are not
my own. i'm unable to walk outside
and not think about a child on the other
side of the world without the same
opportunity. i will tell you that i am
different and love with all my soul and
bones. my reality is not where i would
like to be, but i'll tell you something,
it's better than where i've been before.
before the nightmares. before the scars.
before i thought i knew what love was.
now i know those to be lies. everything
before you, before us. i am different
because i am broken. i broke myself and
threw the pieces into the sky, hoping they
would fall somewhere upon a forgiving
place. in order for my life to have taken
this shape, i had to be reconstructed in
the universe's way. finally rising up to see
your eyes, it gives me love and a life i feel
is different, every single day. and if i'm
being honest, we are all broken. some just
find peace within the cracks.

i just want to lie completely naked with you and talk about how we are the ones that love found. not only enjoying the freedoms that come with it, but knowing we are the lucky ones. in a world where relationships often falter and jump off the edge of the earth because commitment is at times an issue, i am committing to you and to us, my life. our bed is not only a playroom for our dreams and desires, it is where we come to worship the words we have been dying to tell each other all day. after we are done for the night, i will wake up and make sure you are taken care of before you open your eyes.

not because you cannot take care of
yourself, but because i love you and
with those words comes a responsibility
to uphold. i take pride in that and it's the
most important thing in my life.
making damn sure you are protected is
something i will give my life to. for you
and only you will i spend my energy on
your safety and letting your soul be free.
because there is nothing worse than
being somewhere your soul is tied to the
body. i will live with you and for you,
until death finally gets to say my name.
until then, your mouth does it perfectly.
there is no one else i'd rather wake up to,
hold and love, than you, sweetheart.

these are my vows to you.

she has her days like most of us,
but she chooses to rise with the
sun and burn without fear of failing.

it's remarkable considering all of the
hard times that have found her.
she doesn't give up. she doesn't know
how to. she stands tall and plays with
the stars knowing she can go to them
whenever she needs to.

her heart listens to the wind and feels it
running free through her soul. a vibrant
woman, full of flowers and books,
who can be a hurricane when tested and
a sunday morning breeze, even when
things aren't going her way.

she sleeps with her mind open to the
universe and is the dream catcher for the
moon. she's been like that ever since the
night she was born.

some people
may call us lost,
but we always
know that home
is only a touch away.

for when a breath is
taken, love should be
given.

i'm sorry i can't give you more.
you deserve so much. just know
what i have to give is what's left of
decades of unbearable pain and
unclaimed dreams. it's not beautiful.
it's not something many would want.
i'm ashamed of it most of the time.
all of the things i've given to those who
then turned around and left because it
wasn't enough, i wish i had realized it
was a blessing. the way they burned their
name on my heart and thought i would
be fine, it was at my own doing. i allowed
it, because i thought i deserved that love.
it's hard to know the difference when you
don't love yourself the same. after all of
these years, i can finally say i am okay.
every once and a while i feel it beat
differently, but i know it's because i am
still growing as a man. i'm still here and
learning how to walk with these new feet
underneath me. every day is a challenge,
but it's the challenge that makes us
become who we are born to be. and the
sad thing is, i've missed so much because
i had been running through everything,
hoping my past wouldn't catch up to me.

all of the things i ever thought i lost in my
life, you've always held them inside of you.
and to think, people spend their whole
lives going mad, trying desperately to
search and lift up the earth in search of
finding these pieces of themselves.

when in fact, it's never actually lost at all.
it's held tightly in the arms of a breathing
soul, looking for the same things.

"it's important you know."
she said it as if time itself
was waiting for her to finish
her thought. it made me stop
and turn to her and ask,
"important i know what, my love?"

she smiled like only the oceans know how
on a rainy day and said, "that you never
forget the reasons you hold onto the rose
long after the petals fall to earth. we all
die, but the things we leave behind will
one day grow and become what we always
dreamed living could be like. we are more
than our tears. we are more than our
blood. we are more than the flesh that
wraps around our bones. we are human,
and to be human means having a love for
everything, but knowing the difference
between letting go for yourself,
and holding on because of guilt."

with her tender eyes closed, she told me,
"all i want is blue sky." i did everything i
could to move the clouds with my hands
and heart. finally i whispered, "open your
eyes. you need to see this." placing my
arms around her fragile body,
we both had our eyes on the same thing,
as we held together the sky. holding her,
i knew i was holding everything i would
ever need. i told her, "where we go from
here might not be the destination we
want, but it will lead us to where we need
to be. do not be afraid, sweetheart, for the
sun will follow our steps. even if our
shadows are dancing from a distance,
they are lovers as well and know how to
find each other in the dark. you are my
blue sky, darling. you've always been since
the rain started to sing your name as it
washed over my sins. you move, i move.
you breathe, i breathe. i trust in us with
all i have ever been through. i survived
everything i thought should have killed
me. now i know the reasons why i wear
these scars. without them, there is no you.
there's no us." and so we sat there on the
edge of forever, looking at life for the rest
of the night... just holding each other
together.

my eyes have seen childhood friends pass
before they were given a chance to live a
life for themselves. it still haunts me
today. i could've done more. my eyes have
seen a broken home with brothers who
didn't know where to run, but finally
found shelter from it all, underneath a
rising sun. i could've done more. my eyes
have seen a war, where a band of brothers
went to hell and fought the devil and his
demons in order to try and make a
difference. we tried our hardest. my eyes
have seen love blossom across state lines
and through the stars at night. i know
this by the way the moon always smiles
back at me. we are doing our best.
my eyes have seen the grand canyon,
statue of liberty, and lighthouses on
each side of

the coast. my eyes have seen hope in the shape of your heart and in the way my soul cannot stop touching yours. when i tell you that you are the most beautiful thing they have ever seen, you need to believe me. and now you know my eyes have been baptized by the purity of which lives inside of you. even the darkest of places you think you have, i see love breaking over the horizon as if a new day is being born. i know i'm a lucky man. a man who is able to play in your light and taste its flavor.

i'll never stop drinking from it.

she loves with a love of her own.
she has a few tattoos that symbolize
the freedom she has tasted before,
but they only tell half the story of
what makes her who she is.
whatever she does, it never seems to
be enough, or the one she is with.
they single out her heart, as if it is the
one at fault. she laughs, says a few choice
words to them, turns, and leaves before
giving anymore time to a lost cause.

she tells herself, "those who wish to be
free, cannot allow gravity to keep them
from breathing in the stars."

you are too beautiful for me.
from the way your hair falls on
your shoulders, it reminds me of
the mountains catching the sun
after being up for too long. from the
way you smile so perfectly, it makes
my heartstrings sing and come violently
undone. the way you close your eyes has
mine hoping they never close again. you
are so unique in the way you make your
noises; the little ones you don't think i
can hear, but do, and i love every single
one.

you are too beautiful for me. from the way
you say my name and make my soul fall to
its knees. to the clothes you wear that you
don't think are sexy, but in my eyes are
amazing for any occasion. to the way you
sleep and how you make my body shake,
hoping i will be able to

hold you in a different way than men
have in the past. i have never met a
woman who has made me so nervous
or personally made myself think i don't
deserve them. but seeing you the way i
do, i can honestly say you are so much
more than i deserve. i have never seen a
woman who could or ever will match your
glowing soul. i have never seen a woman
like you before in my life and it scares me
that i may not be enough for you. you are
too beautiful for me. you are too beautiful
for even the stars. you, my dear, you are a
kind of magic for those who would start
believing in it if they ever saw you the way
i do.

she is far from normal and has a gift for

seeking out adventures so many have

reluctantly passed on. she is fearless in

the eye of life and can make a grown man

cry. not because she wants to, but because

they tried to do it to her first.

it's important to her that her happiness is

met daily, regardless of her situation.

sometimes when the night is right,

she lets loose the wild inside of her crazy

heart and dances with it.

and on those occasions, there's no such

thing as last call...

only memories to be made.

there are people who venture across
your path and for some reason, you
know without question, or hesitation
they are meant to better your life in some
capacity. though at times we are uncertain
of our very own footsteps, they provide us
with a reassuring feeling we are right
where the universe has claimed for us to
be. it's uncanny how your mind and heart
trust this person without ever knowing
how they will be able to treat you. but you
do because you know it's going to be okay
with them there. in life, we will have
these occurrences and some will trespass
without asking, making you question
your very own existence. that's what life is,
questions without ever getting the right
answers. these people will come out of
nowhere, without warning, only to
catapult your soul into a new beginning.
one you always knew you were worthy of.
and the catch, that awful, bloody, and
unwanted catch is, they leave. you ask
yourself a million times why you let
yourself be open and vulnerable for so

long. you hurt as if the sky had died and
left the moon and sun orphaned to be lost
forever. you're constantly roaming for
closure until someone else comes along
and makes you appreciate yourself for the
heartache they have shared before you.
only to tell you that they too have seen
the wonders of the unknown and how
powerful a conversation is when you
believed all words were lost. it's hard to
accept when you know you two were
meant to love with a never before tasted
kind of love. a constant life doesn't exist.
we are all changing and therefore our
souls will always be on the move until
we find one who can trust the fall. it's an
inside job and we need to stop robbing
ourselves of that gift. treat those people
kind. water them if they need it.
and above all else, never forget those
who saw the very best of you when you
thought you had nothing left to give.
whether they stay or leave, the time spent
is familiar to you, because they knew you
before your heart was caged.

she made it.
some don't understand how she pulled
it off, but she did. over time the clouds
started to fade away and gave way to
multiple suns. showering her with all of
the love needed to be happy and all the
warmth one hopes to find in every hug.
being alone is hard and it's not for
everyone, but it is for those who need to
find their smile again. that's the keyword,
again. some will only see it when it
benefits them, while others find it in the
ones they love every day. and she has
done it beautifully by finally finding it
within herself. she wears it with
sunglasses and sandals when the weather
is right. other days when a bit more
sophistication is called for, she wears the
moon with it. she made it and continues
to make it because of her belief that love
is more than just being present where the
meaning is a sometime feeling.

she often challenges herself to try
different things and get better at what
she is already good at. she knew she had
to if there ever came a time when things
got out of hand, she would need to be
able to control it. it's in those moments
we find ourselves and who we really are.
it's paramount for growth and stability
within our bones. she stayed with it and
conquered all of her fears that had been
accumulating over the years. a spiritual
cleanse of all the leftovers holding onto
what was no longer theirs. she always
finds a way to push herself by knowing
failing is never an option. she will sweat,
cuss, and bleed before ever thinking
about quitting. it's not who she is.
her resilience has kept the wolves in her
life from attacking her confidence.
those negative thoughts only feed on the
weak and she has a warrior's mentality
that is always in the fight. it's what keeps
her from being like the rest. she's a lion
amongst the sheep. one that shows her
teeth when others are running from those
who think they own everything they see.

when our hands were interlocked,
i knew it was a place i never wanted
to leave. it's more than just a home
for me...

it's the bridge for our souls.

she can't tell her heart to love, just as
she can't listen to her mind when it tells
her the truth. she's good at being lonely,
but fakes the smile to get by. she used to
laugh at the jokes and dance when the
floor was empty. now she's at a table full
of things she can't have, waiting for her
song to be played. she can't stand being
this way, but it helps when you're getting
stronger by the day. she can't tell him she
loves him, when being alone is how she
feels. knowing how much it hurts and
feeling half-broken and alone, she exited
the room that had once been her rescue.
no goodbye was said and when she left,
she left behind the woman he had tried to
change. a woman he thought had been
dead. you can't change the heart of the
wounded. you can only hope they don't
see you again. a half-broken woman is
still as powerful as any whole man who
tried to break her.

i love you, because you allowed me
to swim to your shores and finally
rest when everyone else was trying
to push me back out into the chaos
i used to be.

you provided me with something no one
else was willing to give. within seconds i
had found a feeling of trust and a place to
watch the seasons change around us.

as we both let go of the breath we had
been holding onto, the moon and sun
began to dance again.

she chased the rainbows and
never once was after the gold.

for her, it was merely about the
feeling of being alive and finding
herself at the end of it.

there's no greater treasure in this
world than knowing you are made
from the things you believe in.

i never want to change your
world. i just want you to be
the moon in mine.

there's a certain feeling you get
when you know you're around
someone created to be more
human than one could ever be.

the love in you, brings out the best
in me. we've met before, sweetheart.

a time when our bodies had
yet to be married to our souls.

she fell more times than she flew,
but it was all in the way she loved.
she gave her name to life and with
that, she knowingly sacrificed for
the stars. in order to become who
she became, she knew it would be
a tumultuous task. all things come
at a price, and so she keeps her
dreams alive by empowering her
mind to believe one day the steps
that led her to where she is, will
turn out to be the light needed
for the ones who seem hell-bent
on staying grounded. for some,
it's what they define living to be,
but she's not one to listen to those
who have never bled for what they
wanted from it.

i wish i could put the world in my pocket
for a little while and make all of your
worries disappear. i can see the tears on
the back of your throat. the ones that are
running, trying to hide from the sun.
and when i present it back to the universe,
i'll make sure to ask for a few more stars,
just for you. time does not always heal
and fresh wounds are hard to conceal
when living in a place filled with so much
unknown. but please listen to me, my
love, when i say whatever happens today,
i will be holding you until our bodies turn
to dust and our souls become one. we all
begin to die at birth, and you were the
one meant for me to find to survive the
fall. even when i was lost and abandoned
in the dark, i knew i would find you,
because i have had the world in my
pocket before.

sometimes, it's all in the way you undress
her that tells her all she needs to know
about you.

and darling, ever since we have started
to become us, my mind undresses you
a thousand times every day, before my
hands even think about touching you.

i knew when we met that i was either
going to die with you, or die a little each
day without you. love comes to all of us
at some point in our lives, whether we are
ready for it, or not. and when it hits you,
everything stops for a few seconds so you
can take in the entirety of the moment.
i talk to the moon each night and she
gives me some secrets about you. some of
the things you've been through, and what
you are dealing with now. i promised not
to say anything, but i feel you the most at
night, and it's then i realize that i have
found the one we all hope crosses our
path. the one who stays because they
choose to. the one who makes you
appreciate everywhere you have been and

all of the bullshit you've had to endure.
there are no mistakes, because timing is
everything. it's what makes a day last
forever. i have that with you. i also know
there's a possibility of it not working out.
it is how life keeps the balance of the stars
at night. we do not always get what we
want. we only get what we need in order
to become the reason for our existence.
no matter where the moon rests,
your story is safe.

she is the best listener when it comes
down to knowing how hard love can be
and how beautiful it is to rise and fall
each night to see the one you love just
for that moment of understanding
to know you're exactly where you need
to be.

when you're tired and feel like
staying down, just know i'll be
the bridge to bring you back.

she understands the
value of conversation
so well. even when there
are no words spoken,
you can tell she means
everything she says.
do not be with someone
who thinks silence is a bad
thing. if silence makes them
uncomfortable, they have
been with too many that have
conformed to their ways. she is
highly opinionated in the eyes
of many, but the way she explains
how two glasses of wine on a friday
night helps her heart, you listen
intently, because you know after the
second one, a bottle of memories will
be shared. it's all about the way she
makes you feel by being herself.

as if the morning waited on the
conversation to end, just so that
you could experience such
euphoria.

i'll probably never hold you just
right when you need it the most.
i'll probably never kiss you like
i should when the time calls for it.
i'll probably never say your name
the way you whisper mine, but i'll try.
i am flawed, but in the most honest
form. love has shaped me and cut into
my bones, so i will try to be all of what
has never been given to you in your life.
i promise you, i will try harder than the
ones before me. you not only deserve it,
you encompass all the things i've never
had the honor of knowing. you are unique
beyond description. you are masterfully
handmade from a single star. one that i
wished upon before my body new my
name. it's been you, and will always be
you who i open and close my eyes to see.
no matter if the night tries to take you
away from me. no matter how far the
distance is between our fingertips,
i will give you the parts of me that have
been hiding, patiently waiting for
someone to finally recognize i too,
am human.

i never knew much about life when i was younger. i say that now being thirty, but feeling fifty. my body has been through so much and i cannot believe my heart is still alive to try this crazy spectacle called love, one more time. i never knew much about giving someone your best. growing up with divorced parents never taught me the phrase, but it did teach me how not to be. humans make mistakes, that's a given. i just wish i would've been given a better act to follow. i never knew much about how to live, laugh, and love. i've had many attempts in the past, but i was missing something. looking back on my time here on earth, it's hard to grasp the idea that someone can go so long without the one who they have always needed their whole life. love is forever after. that's what life has come to mean to me since the day i met you. i never experienced those things together, because you weren't a part of them with me. it's been right in front of me this whole time. it just took living in the moment of you and i to realize that's all we need in order to spend forever with someone, laugh without knowing why, and love freely without needing a reason.

her life hasn't been the easiest, and i
guess that's why she loves and lives the
way she does. without regret, worry, or
fear from another, her wild heart beats
like thunder. the leaving is always the
hardest, but she controls the situation
the best way she knows how. growing up
we all experience loss at pivotal moments
in our lives that ultimately molds us.
it becomes our dna. we're all made up of
regret, pain, love, and the unforeseen
absence of others. be it by choice or the
universe saying, "you are no longer
needed now. you can finally go home and
rest for a while." she has always been one
to laugh when others cry and cry when no
one is watching. her emotional side
hardly ever presents itself, but you know
what, that's okay. she is sincere

when she needs to be and fights not only
for her right to speak, but to love whoever
she wants. she doesn't see faces, she sees
hope. she doesn't hold just anybody,
only reciprocating souls. her life is not
for the weakhearted. it's for someone
who believes in her and stands for and
beside her when the world is trying to
tell her to fall in line with the rest of the
faceless names. i promise you she is
stronger than you. if you are not going
to be there for her, it's not a problem.
she's had worse things happen to her
than someone breaking a promise.
but just know after she breaks,
she will become the fire you now see
dancing around the sun.

she'll be okay. she's been to hell
a few times before you anyways.

please hear me, sweet one, when i tell
you they will try their best to belittle
you and make a fool of you for not
being who they want you to be. it's a
nasty and cruel world out there. a world
that is always changing and shaping the
minds of the ones who follow the
guidelines of how to find the answers.
please hear me, sweet one, when i tell
you all of this is just a rehearsal; a timed
placement for the weak. do not be like
them. never be like those who wish to
change you. i beg you from the bottom of
my soul, please don't let them. you are too
much like the sun; you burn with every
chance you're awake. continue to spill
into the sky with the colors created from
turning hate and pain into love, and value
for the truth. you are different, but in the
most

believable form. there's nothing fake or two-face about you. that's why they will try their hardest to take your heart and present it as a trophy for others who dare to fly off the grid. your destination has never been planned nor will it ever be a place you call home for longer than needed. it's okay to wander amongst the stars. it's when one becomes complacent that they take you and turn you into a number. you are too ambitious for them and for that reason alone, you must continue to evolve into the wildflower you've always been. please hear me, sweet one, when i tell you to dance with the wind and be free. become all that you've been destined to be;

a leader and liberator for the universe.

the way she made her broken heart
whole again by loving herself more
each day, not only transformed her
into the woman she is now, but it
taught the earth how to find beauty
within the cracks left behind by those
who abused it. she stays devoted to her
craft of creating hope for those who
swear there's none left. not all angels
look the same, but they are born to do
incredible things. self-love is the most
powerful weapon there is. one can
never have enough. when you think
there is nowhere left to go,look up and
you will see a million reasons why falling
is in fact the most beautiful way to fly.

for in that moment is where you'll find
your true-self.

she walks with her eyes on her heart,
because she knows how easy it is to lose
your mind over someone. empowered by
the stars inside her soul, she takes on life
and everything that stands in her way.
don't be surprised if you get left behind
while she is around. she is created from
the winds given off by the moon when it
whispers to the universe. no matter what
she's been told, not all flowers bloom the
same. this one time, she was planted in a
bed of lies and came out smelling of the
truth for those who tried to take her shine.
without having gone through what she
did, her appreciation for the breath she
breathes would not be as it is today.
each deep breath is a sign that she's
fighting. each deep breath exhaled is a
sign she won. sometimes we don't get to
experience what it's like to be alive while
having a beating heart. she does her best
to make each one count, even when
others are counting her out. she's been
tested and continues to prove why living
life your own way will always be the right
answer to the questions being asked by
those in the crowd behind you.

there's this story about a young butterfly who had her wings plucked from her a long time ago. she was misunderstood and no one wanted to see the beauty she was born with. she tried so hard to be accepted and loved by others, but she was made to stand out when the rest were made to fit in. she would look to the sky as the ones who punished her took flight with grace and determination to outshine the sun raining down on the earth below. she never gave up and continued on despite the fact she had been handicapped by the ones she thought would always be there for her. a few years passed and out of nowhere, she began to grow a new set. she had moved on from the rest of the pack and started to enjoy the things she became accustomed to.

unsure of how or why, she was going to take full advantage of the gift being given. little by little, she grew into her wings and the colors made the roses and dandelions jealous. she shows hope by flying to each one so they know love comes from everything that is willing to live without things others take for granted. so that they know perseverance can turn a struggle into a victory. all things are created to be recognized for what they are. the butterfly has seen days where even her wings weren't enough to catch the breeze. she would sit on the petals and listen to the birds sing, wishing it could make the music heard by so many. she studied the light around it.
she's smarter than the rest.
she figured out you don't have to be heard to be seen and admired by many.
a single butterfly changed the world and in doing so, changed the way they now fly.

she isn't really that complicated.
though at times that sentence itself
isn't entirely true. she doesn't waste
time on those who do not care to pay
attention to details and her favorite
books. it takes effort. it takes you
wanting her more than the oceans wish
to constantly fall in love with the shores.
you need to ask questions. don't be the
one to think he knows and is too proud
to ask. you will look like a fool and she
will point that out to you in case you
think otherwise. be kind. be gentle.
she is looking for a lover of not only the
confident kind, but a heart that values
touch and conversation. if you think you
aren't giving your best to her, you don't
have to ask yourself again, because you

know what it takes to hold onto someone
this special. if you should be egotistical,
someone will be thanking you when you
thought you'd be better off without her.
now your silly and childish self will be
looking for her in everyone else. all you
will find is her laugh, and it will drive
you crazy, but i tried to warn you.
a woman like her is a slow beautiful
death for some and a heart attack for
others. it all depends on how you want
to be remembered. if you cannot stay,
please, do not trick her into thinking
you will. you won't only regret that
decision, you will wish you didn't make
an enemy of her caliber. there are no
white flags when it comes to lying to
her. she's already killed you twice before
you said hello.

some people don't get her and why she
acts the way she does. she knows her
style isn't meant for everyone and that's
perfectly fine for the trailblazer she is.
whether it's in high heels or flip flops,
she can conquer any task. she doesn't play
well with those who only hear what they
want. being honest with yourself is the
first step in becoming successful, so she
aims every day to be the best version of
the woman others have incessantly tried
to tell would never succeed. her no filter
approach at life sets her apart from those
who have never questioned a damn thing.
an excuse will never exit her mouth.

too many of those already exist around
her. she wasn't born to please an audience,
because she always has an ace up her
sleeve. she makes her own stage each time
she opens a new door in her life. we tend
to only understand the things we know,
and for that reason alone, her life is a
mystery embodied by a question mark
she proudly wears. life isn't about
pleasing others. its about making sure
you're happy with who you are and what
you stand for. even if she's alone in that
belief, you will never see her willing to
compromise who she is for what you
think she should be.

you are never going to find someone who loves you like i do. who takes your tired body into their chest and plays with your hair the way you like it. who will go out to get you something when you don't feel like getting up. who will talk to you in the most gentle and loving way when we disagree on something, or laying on the couch being lazy. who will tell you how death has been put to sleep, because you've made me concentrate on living more than worrying about it as much. who will stand beside you and watch the sky catch fire while we kiss the universe back to life. i say these things because i want you to know how much i love you and will do anything for you. not because it's what you ask of me, but it's what i ask of myself to give to you. and if something should happen, sweetheart, to where we are no longer holding life together, just know i hope you find someone that can do these things for you and with you. please do not accept anything less than love in all the places you crave it.

and when
the stars call,
please do
not go too far.

i've been
waiting my
whole life for
this feeling.

she lays on her back with her heart in her throat. it's been a struggle for her to speak of life and formulating words so that others can comprehend her situation. the pain is overwhelming, but it's a feeling needed nonetheless. a kind of pain she has tolerated going on a few years now. like most of us, the one thing she can't handle is someone leaving when they had said, "always meant forever." today she found herself on two feet. today she found the emotions needed to walk away. not only from who she had been, but the memories created through passing stars. this is her test. one where giving up doesn't exist. she's checked off all the boxes in her head. she's attempting to put one foot in front of the other for all who have told her to rest. life may have found her at her weakest, but it will not define her. so here she stands, walking on dreams made of broken glass, ready to fight for her life. nothing makes you appreciate your journey more than finding love within yourself and planting it where others said it would never grow.

when she let her hair down,
stardust falls to the floor.
her strength is on full display
as she conducts the universe
and helps those understand
the sounds surrounding the
lonely.
her mission in life is to show
others that a woman's ambition
is nothing to mess with. if you
think otherwise, you've obviously
never met any of her
girlfriends.
her mind is a garden, growing new ideas
each morning. she's a beautiful reason for
all of the unexplained. at times, you just
have to take in the madness in order to
appreciate the darkness one gets
consumed by.
we all have it, and she uses it to her
advantage when others cannot see
through it.

when i saw her,
all of what had
tried to take me
before was now
gone.

  i sleep with rivers
  no longer violently
  thrashing against
  my eyes. i rest my
  entire life next to
  her, and it is all
  removed.

and then i heard her laugh.

it was in that split second i
knew i never wanted to die.

all i could do was hope to give
back to her as much as she had
so effortlessly given to me.

she has goals set for her life that
reach out beyond the depths of
time and space. her aspirations
are to be the best at everything
she does. some have laughed at
such a notion, but they don't
even believe in themselves,
and she knows it. we all have
come across those people.
the ones who can't fathom the
thought of ever being more than
a last name and face in society.
she's all heart, all the time. no rules
can define her and hates staying
in-between the lines. a body
filled with her own share of
heartache and second guesses,
she chose to be more and chooses
the freedom that comes with it.
her happiness is her favorite accessory,
and it goes good with anything she wears.

she wears red lipstick and kisses
the words before she speaks. a deadly
combination if you get on her bad side.
she doesn't play favorites and knows how
to make an entrance even when she leaves.
her drink of choice is honesty and will at
times drink a little more than she should,
but that's just the fight in her. it will never
be replicated. she will be your own worst
enemy if you believe you are smarter than
she is. her softer side consists of good
music and the top down.

it's her road and we are all just passing by.

she's messy, but in the most gorgeous
way. she will take your heart when you
least expect it, because she can. it's not
her being malicious, it's her being
everything you never thought existed.
she has a backbone and power that the
sun uses to rest on. she has grace and a
kiss so powerful the night uses it to the
light the sky. she doesn't make excuses for
who she is. if others find it unattractive or
overbearing than they have been standing
in the same spot for too long.

you have to move with her to keep
up. she's not a runner from things.
she accepts all challenges while
maintaining her distance from people
who can't understand the essence of
being authentic.

when i first saw her breathe,

i knew i could finally let go of the

breath i had been holding onto for

so long.

when i am absent from you.
when my soul cannot touch
yours. when my bones are
afraid to move because you
are not here, it's another type
of hell for me.

all of my fears come after me at
once. i am not afraid of being alone,
but to know you are gone while i am
still breathing, i become like a child
who never believed in ghosts until
they came kicking down my door.

when love enters your life and
rearranges your dreams to make
them a walking reality, you walk
with it.

she is beautiful.
not because countless people tell
her, but it's the way she loves herself.
not many can do it day in and day out
after the tears fall at night and the heart
screams during the quiet moments.
she keeps it all together, but it doesn't
mean her headaches from yesterday go
numb. it's a powerful thought to know
you have the ability to be who you want
every day you open your eyes. she takes
that in full stride and runs to edge of the
world with it. she gathers her tears, plants
them in the sky, and watches new stars be
born because of the pain she had to face
and overcome. she's beautiful, and to be
that after hell has been your home for a
while, it's a phenomenal piece of jewelry
for your soul to wear; especially when you
can see it in her eyes. conquering her own
hurt and sadness makes you forget about
them living in your life. she's a healer of
not only the broken, but the ones who
think they aren't.

do not force her to be what you
want. do not think you can change
her mind when it comes to ordinary
things in life. she doesn't think like
you, or for that matter, act like you.
she's extraordinary because of the love
she's invested in herself. you cannot look
at art and try to manipulate it into being
what you think it should be. life doesn't
work like that and neither does she.
admire her for what she represents and
value her worth. her masterpieces will live
on the walls of your heart and soul.
she's an artist painting with words she
has learned from the stars. she's a
sculpture made from the flowers and sea
shells she has collected. when you try and
push her back against the wall, she will
bury you with the rubble. she's a builder
of what others have tried to use against
her. a lesson she learned while climbing
the mountains others had put in front of
her.

she may be a queen, but underneath
the crown she wears is a yearning for
a meaningful life. in order to conquer
your adventures, some need to fly
alone. so she dropped her crown and
picked up her wings. the stronger the
winds, the more wild she became.

now she is flying with freedom.

when asked about her when she's away away, he said, "life is nothing more than wasting breaths and being somewhere you do not wish to be when she is not here. she's a life i never thought i would get to live."

it's easy to get lost in the world
when the universe spins you
around so many times in search
for an answer you never knew was
there, until she made you stop and
finally believe in yourself when you
had been born with a blind heart.

souls understand souls extremely well.

it's the human contact of those who

choose to belittle the other that

oftentimes interrupts and mangles the

balance of power within ourselves.

when was the last time you fell apart for
something?

when was the last time you broke a bone
on a dream you had?

when was the last time you were lying in
bed, completely inebriated by the
universe?

i hope you search the corners of every
piece of desire you have consumed in your
life, and when you get through with your
discoveries,

i hope it isn't the last time you try to
understand yourself.

please do not apologize to me for being who you are. i am not him. i accept and adore you as you are. please do not think i am better than you, because i am not. whatever he said to you, or however he treated you, i will not be that malicious and carefree with someone so kind and sincere. i come with love and only love for you, sweetheart. we are all formed from somewhere and eventually return when we are ready. we do that so we can see the growth of our hearts in hopes of finding someone to share that common place with. i wish to only know you better and hold your hand as much as i can until my body is at rest with love buried in my chest and words that do not necessarily define me, written above me. a hundred miles or a thousand miles, i am always whispering your name to the moon.

we go back a ways, and she still owes me a few favors.

my tears tell a story
of how a man was
swallowed by the
ocean inside of him,
only to be released by
the love swimming in
your heart.

i wish i could
promise you
something as
sure as life has
promised us
death.

she tries so hard to make ends meet.
it almost seems like nothing will ever
fall into place. but it doesn't deter her
from being who she needs to be for
those around her. there's something
special about her and how she continues
on against the onslaught of negativity she
faces. in her world, the cape never comes
off. she always gets what she wants
because that's just who she is. do not talk
down to her when speaking about life and
love. she's experienced both more than
you've had heart beats. it's all about
balance, and that means making sure her
glass is always full. if you have a reason for
not believing in her, you'll regret it. you
see, not everyone can swim underwater
while breathing life into the sea.

she's not the normal kind.
she's different, and if you ask her why,
she would tell you, it's because not every
star truly dies. those that cannot be seen
are the ones who shine the brightest.
she didn't change, she just adjusted her
vibe and the world shifted. where there
were tears, her eyes are now clear without
fear of falling asleep. she anticipates the
next day with her soul on her sleeve and
her bed nicely made. it happens once you
stop settling for what others say you are
worth. it's all background noise.
after promptly realizing what had to take
place, she saw her face in the mirror for
the first time without the dread that had
been following her around all of her life.
she had been someone else for so long,
it almost ruined her. catching a glimpse
of greatness is all it takes for the rest to
follow you. it took her a little longer than
she wanted, but the universe has a hard
time understanding the supernatural
when it comes in human form.

to live in love, one becomes more than
a soul. they become a reason and answer
to those who question the meaning of
a purposeful life. time doesn't always
decide what happens. it's either the
heart, or the mind most of the time.

do not let it kill what you truly feel,
and do not overthink something you
know isn't worth the struggle. let it go
or hold it forever.

there's no in-between when it comes to
happiness.

she made dancing with the moon a
simple feat. the secret was always
having the world at her feet.
darkness was her friend when she was
young, it taught her how to see the stars
in everything that was numb. her eyes
have seen first hand what it takes to get
what you need in life. she is her own hero
for the obstacles she's had to overcome.
it's not easy when you feel like you're the
only one who isn't against you. in order
to become who you are meant to be,
you have to let go of those holding the
rope and finally taste a bit of freedom.
we all fall, some just do it more
beautifully than others. she was born to
feel the sun rise and set, even if it meant
picking up pieces of a shattered world
half her life. there's no fear in those who
have fallen. only more adventures will
cure the pain for a dancing spirit.

when you are with her, stay naked
in love. trust comes in the form of
many things, but a woman who
undresses her fears in front of you
is someone you should never leave.

it has taken her years to be vulnerable.
don't ruin her because you are afraid of
being human.

there's a quietness and calmness when
the soul is at rest. it's not mad anymore.
it's not determined to find the negative
holes of the skin. it sits with its hands
on the heart of those in pain. do not be
afraid when something you cannot
explain happens. be content in the
understanding that the soul is in
fact the hope within the lining of the
universe we all search for. take a look
inside from time to time.

all the answers are there.
they always have been.

her tears over the years have matured.
they now water the wounds of her flowers
instead of flooding the streets of her
world. keep in mind these are the same
ones she had kept out of view from those
close to her. she was not afraid of being
judged. it was about her pride telling her
to never give up. tears are not a weakness.
only those who judge are the cowards.
waking up one morning after using the
pillow as a shield against the universe,
she noticed several spots had turned into
pearls. even in the dark, the things we
think are ugly and depressing, grow from
the stars inside our bones. we are all
spectacular and needed by someone.
a tear is so much more than just a feeling.
it's the soul's way of watering the scars we
ourselves cannot see.

not every girl is created from
broken smiles and cracked hearts,
but she pulled it all together lovingly.
she's the universe's child, aligning the
stars in her favor for the hope that now
resonates in her soul.

she is human and that's what
makes her beautiful. a lot of
people try to be, but she does
it with ease.

a smile like hers can bring the
universe back together when
the stars are lost.

on the outer edge of this world is where lovers are willing to make a promise to each other. i hope to meet you there so we know what pain meant when it told us both, "no, not now."

she is recklessly beautiful in all the ways that make her unattainable for simple minded fools. you have to be on her level of crazy and free. it won't work if you're unwilling to open your mind to the possibility of dying a little just to be with her. she will be able to bring you back to your mind once you jump from the moon with her. just when you think she is incapable of testing your will to be yourself, you'll be right next to her, swinging on the stars of where she used to play as a child. she doesn't have a home where she rests her soul. her body may be asleep, but the rest of her is all about finding that next feeling of wonderment. it truly is captivating the way she can close her eyes, but still be more alive than humans thought possible. there's no time for sleep when you're busy exploring the origins of what makes you who you are.

she looks at him, wishing he could see the
pain growing from her heart. he sits there,
looking at her, looking at him, thinking if
she can tell it's over. a truth both can see,
but neither can honestly say.

sometimes, we put ourselves through
misery for the betterment of others,
only to be rewarded with getting out
half-alive.

they tell her she used to be a lot of things,
but the one thing she has remained is
true to herself; a mountain of everything
beautiful and sacred. when she walks,
the universe spins around to take notice.
she has other mountains running towards
her, hoping to be like her one day.
there's a healing power she has.
when they ask her what her secret is,
she explains to them how an abused
and tortured soul found light in the
darkest of rooms in her heart, even when
the doors had an easy time opening.
there are locks on all of her windows
now, but every once and a while she lets
them open to air out all of the stars she
keeps safe at night.

a
love
for
her,
means
a
love
for
all
i
do.

if you're only interested in her for what's
between her legs and not what's in her
heart and mind,

you're going to find out why you will
never be able to handle a woman like
her.

show me a woman with scars and tell me
she isn't the most beautiful thing your
eyes have ever rested on.

if you think otherwise, take a look at the
moon and try to tell me the same thing.

she is not of this world and doesn't act
like the rest. she's a wild card and won't
apologize for being that way anymore.
acceptance is key when it comes down
to finding out who will be there for you
when you are in need of yourself.
her reflection is pure and her mind is
hungry. her smile lifts the clouds on rainy
days. she is a revelation of love and chaos.
if you do not comprehend what she offers,
she isn't waiting around for excuses from
you. she's already heard them before,
and now respects herself enough to not
be an option. she is okay with being alone.
one time, someone mistook her love for a
temporary affair, and now her dreams and
ambitions keep her warm.

she is strong, because of how she holds
the sky together when everyone around
her seems to be falling apart. her hands
have traces of the stars and is a map of
the soul within each one. it takes every
breath she has to get the task done,
but she's breathing fire and courage.
over time, her heart has bled and
pumped life for those who told her
they loved her, then left without saying
a single word. it doesn't matter to her
anymore. she's done with people who
only see themselves in the mirror when
they are standing next to her. she has
been tested by her fair share of heartless
individuals, and yet still walks this earth
unscathed. the true test of a person's
character is how well they treat those who
break their spirit by doing nothing at all
except cause them pain. if you intend to
do that, she will leave your heart on the
stake.

there is magic in the stillness.
it's a tragedy so many go without
it and are constantly bombarded
with chaos. we as humans value love,
respect, peace, and a sense of meaning.
your eyes see more when the heart is free
of the chains and ropes we tend to tie to it.
it's not meant to be kept in the dark from
all the things you crave. let it free and
allow it to roam the empty places that
have been left by so many who borrowed
it with intentions on giving it back better
than they found it. i am far from perfect.
i do not live my life as others see fit.
i make a million mistakes within a single
breath, but it is within that single second
of ignorance i fall on something beautiful.
the ability to learn and see things in a
different focus is what separates us as
individuals. you never have to, but i hope
you do not use the same crayon to color
all of your pictures.

she asked, "why do you say the things you do, knowing the possibility of us never being together?"

i took her heart in my hands and spoke to it as if it were my own, "if death were to visit me and ask the same thing, it knows it's inevitable. just as you and i are, sweetheart."

pointing to my own heart, i told her, "this is what we use to die for someone. we sacrifice so much every day if we believe it to be worth the pain and joy it brings. when i tell you all of my breaths from this point forward will be used to keep your stars alive, i mean it."

she would sit outside and watch the
sunrise until tears began to gently fall
like snowflakes on the barren trees.
this act of love is something we all take
for granted, and she took it all in with
such profound attention. it presented
her with sheer conviction to rise again.
she knew if an energy full of its own
heartbreak and pain can continually
kiss the universe each day, she could as
well. it's the immortal hope that lives in
her which proclaims her soul isn't dead
yet; regardless of what they have gone
through together. because of the endless
amounts of new found oxygen that has
grown inside of her, at the end of the day,
she knows without question she deserves
to be loved beyond a reasonable doubt.

we were born with a robe made by
the universe.

we are full of soul and untapped
love.

we may feel naked at times and
utterly frightened by the unknown,

but if we continue on with the
determination of every star used
for our creation, we will one day
find reason for the beating
flower inside of our chest.

she's been through enough games and
babbling lies to know the only thing left
at that point is to move forward.

she believes in life after love. there's no
graveyard to crawl to, only a resting place
to fly from. she has told me before,
"when you are on your back, staring a
hole into the universe, take pieces from
the experience and throw them into the
night without pain. the moon will
understand. whatever you do, don't stop
creating."

what you're going through
right now is important.
love is an extension of a thorn
from the rose. we bleed for
things we do not always need,

> but what it leaves behind teaches
> us that pain is in fact necessary for
> growth. from it, castles are built on
> top of mountains you never
> thought you could reach.

i am sorry for loving you more than you
deserved. i should've known better than
to take the covers from my heart and
throw them away.
it was resting so quietly and minding its
own business. do you know how fucking
long that took?
you can't imagine because you were born
cold and with a spine that only stands for
destruction.
the sad thing is, i am looking across the
room, noticing how casually you're
drinking your wine with your new
heartbreak beside you.
cheers to those who have been left for
dead, only to find life after the storm
had passed and decided not to be a
casualty.
we are all stronger than we think.
even when your heart is beating in the
hand of a magician, the act only lasts for
as long as you believe it to be true.

she doesn't have a religion.

her faith
resides in

the stars, flowers, ocean, and herself.

when she smiled at me, i felt the color of
my eyes change from black to blue.
they were born again inside of those few
seconds, after being destroyed repeatedly
throughout my entire life. it's not easy
looking down at your arms and seeing
words written in lines only a drunken and
depressed man can read. it's not easy
trying to break a mirror on the side of an
already jagged reflection. it's not easy
walking into a church and having people
cast you as a selfish sinner who never
thought about his own actions. it's not
easy when you have finished a bottle of
whiskey and looking for a different chaser
for your demons. it's not easy being me,
but it is easy to love someone who smiles
at you as if you are what they have been
needing. something a little more than fate
brought us to where we are now, and to
say i don't believe in things like that,
is like me saying i don't believe in the
galaxies that have been dancing around
you this whole time i've been holding
you.

he said he wanted to change and be better
for himself. it's been so long since he was
able to do anything he wanted because of
the situations surrounding his life.

it's been difficult, but knowing each day
brings a fresh reflection of the skin he is
wearing, he breathes in the sky and
exhales the dreams he once wished for.
there's something for everyone in this life.
some have to take the detours,
while others drive straight through
without harm. his tattoos, the ones
without color, are not just a story,
they are words he could never say.

her life was formed from bad ideas and
miscalculated risks, but at least she went
for something. there is nothing as cruel in
life as coming to the realization you have
lived for so long without ever taking a
chance. saying that, that's not living.
that's just getting by. her vocabulary
remains intact with, "i can, i will,
and never giving up." not everyone
is built with enough fortitude for failure.
some crumble underneath its name.
she hasn't always been able to fly with her
eyes towards the stars, but once you find
what you fear, you let it drive you. for her,
the fear of not living up to her own

expectations are enough to awake the
sounds of her inner warrior screaming
at her, waking up the bones from
yesterday to grow stronger today.
please do not settle for a few days of the
sun, when you are the sun. please do not
settle for a few nights, staring at the
moon, wishing you could plant your
dreams there when you have always been
the moon. she's calling out to the wild
inside of her to come alive. she knows it's
time to let the fear create her fire and not
destroy the beauty which is inside of her.
run wild, sweet one.

run with all of your soul.

blow open the sky and live there.

you were born for it.

she wanted to be loved like she saw in the movies and read about in her books. a love like her parents had of which she grew up admiring. she wanted to be liked amongst her friends. a group she tried so hard to fit in with. she wanted to have conversations with someone who actually listened to her and heard her opinions about life and the universe. she wanted someone to hold when the nights got cold and the bed turned into a casket where she slowly died each time the moon said, "goodnight." she wanted some type of sign that this is where she was meant to be. a place where she was destined to bloom and become something more than just a human acting as herself. i wish she could see just how much of a monumental impact she has had on the world. not everyone can make the stars dance and fall in love with the honest truth. a truth that screams out how everyone needs to be held from time to time so they know it's okay to shine a little brighter when darkness presents itself.

this morning she said goodbye.
a painful yet accepted exit that was
needed to see through to the other
side. tears marked the floor where she
had once been stone cold and petrified.
living under this roof, she had been
someone else he never wanted her to be.
the way she was able to bend and
transform into herself after taking over
for the moon made her unstoppable.
and he, he was finally replaceable.
looking in the windows of where hope
was eventually found and ultimately
destroyed, she discovered a new calling.
today is a day laced with harmonious
laughter and eyes full of pride. she's ready,
because that's what survivors do.
peaceful tides turn in her heart as she
waits patiently, sitting for the stars.
her home has no walls, no confined
spaces.

everywhere she turns, she's greeted with
love.

there's such a powerful lesson in never
giving up, even if she learned it the hard
way. it was something the memory of her
heart never forgot. she used her words
not to damage anyone else, because she
demanded better of herself than those
who continued to diminish her trust.
as complicated as it was to move on with
her life, she knew the power of belief
would allow her to succeed in all the
areas of her world.

she understands the struggle and values
all the tears. there's quiet beauty in the
wild spilled in order to paint the skies
above you and the flowers underneath
you.

it's empowering once you step out of your
own shadow, and become a sea of
strength.

i want to be a part
of your life. if that
means sitting on
the outside and
helping you grow
until i can hold you,
then that's what i'll do.

everything is worth the
wait if your intentions
are pure.

i have a darkness in me only the moon
can love. now i understand why you've
never left me. i do need you just as much
as you need me. i know you'll say you
need me more, but that's a lie, sweetheart,
it always has been. when i said that i am
afraid of the dark, i was not lying to you.
the truth always shines the brightest
when the lights go out.

there are going to be moments when she cries as loud as wolves howling at the moon. when she doesn't want to get out of bed because the world around her is falling down and she will feel safe not moving. when the day passes and she will be turned off to everything around her. when the rain falls and she just sits there and drinks from it because she is thirsty for reason. when the television will be on so that the noise can drown out her heart and mind. when her hair is all over the place and the makeup on her face is running, but not from the tears. it will be from the fear of not being beautiful enough, even with it on.

that's when she will need someone who is willing to go above and beyond their own measures of love. even if she tells you nothing at all, just listen to her.

she wakes up looking like my
best friend, lover, and twin flame.

the epitome of my inspirations
and desires in all of my dreams.

that's how i know whether or
not she ever wears my ring on
her finger, she will always be
the one who i share all of my
secrets with.

i will forever lover her,
because she says the same
things to me.

she's on fire for the sun and moon.
for the stars and oceans. for the people
in her life and herself. this lovely spirit's
inner compass is always spinning, which
makes sense for this beautiful traveler.
in her heart, these words are engraved
by experience: "the greatest tragedy is
not allowing room for growth in actually
living. our minds are always growing.
don't let someone pull you down below
them just because they see you as a
threat." that's the key, not allowing
mistakes and failures to slow you down
in a world full of recycled excuses.

she was made to do incredible
things. you could tell by the way
she tried to fly with two broken
wings. she was persistent like that.
never willing to wait on life to get
better, because in her mind there
was never a right time. always a
"take over the world" mentality,
no matter what was being said.
even if life tried to take her abilities
and spirit way, it was not going to
stop her from discovering something
new about herself. she loved to learn
and could never find a stopping point
to put down what she was reading.
to her, everything had a way of being
irresistible, but she knew when to pull
the cord while others fell heart first.
it's a turbulent balance for some, but
she knew the wrong way to do things
would eventually lead to the right way
as long as she kept moving forward.

she lives for the wild moments and the
unexpected adventures. someone like
her breathes without regret, because
she knows life is too precious to miss
out on anything. she finally put herself
at the top of her own list, and it has made
all the difference. she finds herself in the
books she reads, the music being played,
and bonfires on the beach. she has been
known to get lost in thought, only
because her mind is beautiful, even if
she isn't making any sense.

whatever you think about her, she has
never been one to give a damn about the
judgment of others. she's comfortable in
her own skin, just as a blossoming rose is,
as it makes its way beneath the concrete.
she does the impossible on a daily basis.

she has a way of bringing
the moon out during the
day. a flick of her hair and
the stars move in unison
to smell her fragrance.

she does have her
moments when doing
nothing is exactly what
needs to be done.

and during those
times, she is still doing
more than most.

some will say i don't deserve
you and they are probably right.

but they don't know what i went
through just to tell you, i love you.

i kissed her lips
and it was the first
time i had tasted
pure universe.

because of it, i now
know where you
came from.

she's incredibly brave for not only getting through what had happened to her, but knowing how much more she has to go and still fighting like hell to bring her smile back to life. there's something to be said about a woman who goes that extra mile, knowing it's a lonely place because not everyone has the guts to make it. she approaches each day with a full heart, accompanied by an appetite to be extraordinary. her success isn't determined by how far she gets.

once you've escaped hell, you stop counting the miles and start believing in your hometown love for yourself.

it pains me to see so-called men
disrespect women and put them
down as if they are superior.
i'm sorry some of you have to go
through the bullshit with guys
who will act one way, but are
after something entirely different.
they will never be able to understand
how breaking someone because you
can is the lowest a human can go.

i have zero compassion for morons who
destroy another just to make themselves
feel better. to those who think you're
doing nothing wrong, i hope someone
comes into your world and rips your heart
out without asking. maybe then you'll
actually feel something for the first time
in your life.

she's as busy as the new york city
streets, with a soul as colorful as
an l.a. sunset.
she's not complicated,
just passionate about
keeping her vibe alive.

you've shown me the most damaged of
souls are enough and deserving of love.
the color of the bruises do not tell the
story. it's what's left when the broken
are healed by someone willing to give
more than they receive that tells the
truth. they go into it realizing they
too are hurting, but somehow crying
together stops the pain. humans like
you never existed before in my life,
but you've gained my trust by holding
me together when countless others let
me die without saying a single word.
all i wanted was to be held by another
who cared as completely as i did. all i
wanted was to feel something other than
my tears bleeding back into me. being
alone is a job not everyone is good at.
it deeply saddens me so many have to
experience being employed by it.

thank you for never leaving me when
i had given you the outs to take.
you believed in me before i had told
you i loved you, and because of it,
my wounds are no longer open to the
fear of losing myself again.

she desperately tried to make the best out of each situation that came across her path, but you have to understand how difficult it gets when you're tripping over landmines disguised as apologies. as soon as he turned his back, he forgot about you. you did nothing wrong when you asked where he was. you did nothing wrong when you asked who was on the phone. you did nothing wrong when you woke up in the middle of the night, only to catch him trying to sneak into bed. you, darling, you are everything that is right with this world, but you care too much for those who do not care for themselves. be selfish with your heart and protect it. it will be a lifesaver for someone who values the depth of your soul.

she took being
broken and created
art in all the places
she traveled.
not everyone is able
to fill the cracks with
so much love and light,
but she does it as if she
is holding the moon.

she knew it was important to live for
herself and in her story, she survived
the ending. it didn't take long for her
to realize you cannot give your love to
someone who doesn't know what to do
with it.
she learned over time how to separate
need from want, and with doing so,
managing time was no longer an issue.
once you start valuing your own
happiness over those who continually
hurt you, thinking they will change,
the easier everything else becomes.
it's not being selfish.
it's your moral obligation to be at your
best for you. even if it's out of character
for you to be the more assertive person.
at the end of the day, she became
everything she had been told didn't exist
and transformed into a heroine who
fought for something others relentlessly
tried to kill.

all she did was breathe
    in the stars and exhale
       the light.

that was the thing about her.
    she always proved she could
       by actions, not words.

let love be war.
sharpen your fire
against me.

use whatever
weapon you wish.

and when you come,
be sure to bring enough
soul to match mine.

this one time, a photograph made me
fall in love without hearing her voice
or knowing how well she danced in
the rain. people might call me crazy
or unrealistic, but if you saw how she
smiled at me in it, you would've already
married her. i haven't quite got there yet,
but one day we will have a picture of our
own, with a date and writing on the back
that reads:

"today, you became mine after being in
my heart for so long.
tomorrow, we will wake up together for
the first time.
forever never meant a damn thing to me,
until i took my first breath with you."

there are going to be all kinds of people who will try and steal your magic during your lifetime.

if you show them your heart and they do not return the gesture, it's time to move on.

love is not a glimpse, it is a fixation.

she gave her everything for the wrong
things and now she's making her way
out of the tragedy of who she used to
be. making sure her words are tied
together with truth is paramount for
the betterment of becoming all she
has read about.
she doesn't have favorite characters,
just treasured quotes locked away in
her journal; highlighted and underlined,
they are a road map to her heart.
underneath her bed are remains of the
pieces that had been broken off during
restless nights of crying herself to sleep.
each one is marked with a kiss and a
prayer. religion became a sour taste in
her mouth over the years, but she still
searches for faith. today, the sky cracked
open and out fell a thousand angels
trying to embrace the chaos running
rampant around her. she turned them
all away, because she knew the only one
who could save her was herself. alone in
her bed, she sleeps with her wings
wrapped around her for safety.

she still keeps the window open
for when the wild needs to be felt.

she did a lot of things, but most
importantly, she continued to
choose what was best for her each
day. she stopped worrying about
those who never returned the calls
or messages. she stopped stressing
over the small stuff and learned how
to grow into her full potential.
she finally gave her heart away to herself.
it takes a rare form of strength to be who
she is. even if she has to fake it a little to
succeed and be happy, she will do it.
she's heard the laughs and jokes from
others who think she is in over her head
with a job not meant for women, but you
have to understand her heart has been
pieced back together by sacrifice and her
own two hands. there's nothing she can't
do, because she has already done it before
you saw her and thought you knew her
type.

don't let the smile fool ya kid, there's fire
behind those eyes.

just fall, sweet one.
i promise you, the wings you have
earned will come alive. part of letting
go is trusting the journey, and you have
always been up for any adventure.
looking down i know how big your eyes
must be, but when you are up in the air,
everything else just fades away.
the pain and hurt accumulated over your
years. the tears and screams no one else
heard or saw. the sadness attached to your
bones. it all will leave you. stretch them
far and don't hold onto it anymore.
when it comes to fear, only those who
are brave enough know how to use it
moving forward with their lives.
being scared is normal, and you, sweet
one, you were made for the extraordinary.

she loved too much and
you could see it in the way
she broke her own heart
trying to please everyone
else, before her smile was
free to dance.

this is what it feels like when
love completely consumes you.
the morning comes and i still
have no answers as to how you
are brighter than what's coming
through the window. the night
greets us with the mother of us
all and though we are grown,
we play like kids in every room
of the house. you are the beat
and breath of my life, darling.
you are what encompasses the
very existence of who i've
become.
this is what it feels like to be
consumed by someone you
never thought would walk into
your life. there are still times i
check your pulse and pinch your
arm to make sure my eyes see
what my heart feels. regardless
of how many stars are visible to us,
you are the one i will always wish on.
for better or for worse, and long after
death has finished calling our names,
my energy will be comprised of the love
we made. it will stay beside you, forever
protecting the one thing i loved more
than myself.

if you know her, chances are she has
changed her mind again this morning.
if you know her, you will understand
the struggle of trying to survive in two
feet of water thinking you are drowning.
if you know her, you will be able to tell
how much hell she has been living in by
the way her silence sounds like thunder.
if you know her, you are lucky to have
someone like that in your life. as much
pain as she's in, her love is brave and
courageous.
a woman of her stature hasn't made it
this far without knowing it takes soul
to live a meaningful life.

if you know her, she won't ever forget you.

i have a mind
that is in constant
search of understanding.

if it means tearing myself apart by
the ends of the universe inside of
me, i will if it leads to discovering
the answers i need.

i've been building and rebuilding
myself all my life. i have never been
one to wait around long enough for
a project to finish. some may call
me mad and crazy, but i don't
mind at all.

i find sweet comfort in the storms,
because there's something about a
slow roll of thunder in your chest
and a steady lightning show in your
heart that makes you feel worthy of
the rain.

she wasn't interested
in going down anymore
rabbit holes to catch what
she wanted.

she never desired to be
alice, just someone who
was as brilliant as the stars
that got lost while trying to
find their way through space.

she finally started
to love the pieces
of herself others
had always failed
to touch.

and it has made all the difference.

i would like to just hold you
the entire day and talk about
the most random of things.

a conversation about nothing
will always bring something
new to the relationship.

she came into this world with a delicate
touch and a wild side. you knew she'd be
unbreakable by the way her smile always
shined after the rain. a lover at heart,
her ability to adapt to the circumstances
surrounding her, has turned her into an
assassin for those attempting to break in
and steal what was never meant for them.
she's still working on the color scheme for
her walls, since everyone keeps painting
them with destruction without thinking
how starting over feels. she continues on
because she's never been good at being
miserable. she'd rather be the butterfly
who refused to stay grounded with a
broken wing than the one who others
felt sorry for.

my words are an open casket, with my
mistakes and failures folded neatly
beside them.
coming back from having your prints
taken and leaving black stains on more
than just your clothes can change a
person.
you're lucky not to have ever walked
where i have been, but i do hope you
find yourself happy wherever you decide,
with someone there to keep your pain
company.
when you peer into the box of my
remains, just remember i chose this
life. this life never had a chance to
choose me.
i was too much soul to contain in just
flesh and bone, living underneath the
clouds when i belonged to the universe.

when you send me away, please,
bury me in the sky next to the
dreamers.

she's the type of woman who makes you
feel better about life and the problems
you thought were going on it. she's the
type of woman to actually listen and have
enough heart to say something with
substance when you are done shedding
who you thought you were. after spending
some time with her, not everything made
sense, but it didn't have to anymore.
she has this revolution in her presence
you can't help but want to be a part of.
it's in the way she makes you feel human,
when for so long you had been the
shadow of your own ghost.
if anyone were to ask me who she is,
i would smile and simply say, magic.

there are things i could tell you and
expressions on how to live your life
better, or to its maximum potential.
how to minimize error so you never
have to regret anything before or after
you are finished doing them. how the
likelihood of me meeting someone like
you was a lightning strike i never saw
coming, but felt a thousand miles away.
there are ways i could show you how
incredibly revealing a sunset is to
someone who has been covered by storms
their whole life. if you are to do anything
with your time, i beg you, never second
guess fate and always believe something
absolutely amazing will knock you on
your ass when you least expect it.
some of the most inspiring heartbeats
are felt when someone comes along to
pick you up at exactly the right moment.
live free and breathe in as many
possibilities as you can, while you can.
every day is the right day when opening
your eyes is an option.

she surprised herself
by how easy it was
letting go of someone
who never committed
to anything, not even
their own heart.

it had always been
her choice and hers
alone to make.

and now she's taking care
of her own flowers instead
of worrying about them
going waterless and unkempt.

when she told you she was different
and no was the only answer, it wasn't
an invitation to try again. do us all a
favor, you clowns who think you're
entitled to something that isn't yours,
go back to your circus and hang yourself
with the wire. to all of those reading who
have been victimized and left feeling
alone and broken, i say to you, you're not.
you are strong, brave, and beautiful.
i may not know you at all, but you will
always have a friend who believes in you.
i may not know your story, but i love you.
i may not know if this helps at all, but i
wanted to at least try. it wasn't your fault
and you did nothing wrong.

when six months turns into three,
we can see who doesn't believe in
justice and a life that truly matters.
i wanted you to know that to me,
you are a hero.

please, my love, just stay with me and show me how to use this face of mine to smile.

please, my love, just stay with me and tell me i am more than the words i have yet to find.

please, my love, just stay and allow us to become together in a world gone mad.

please, my love, just stay and i will show you a heart that still works.

it isn't in the best condition, but the best things in life have been thrown away, because they don't work just right.

she is real in every sense of the
word. with her hair flowing past
her shoulders like the grandest of
waterfalls i wish to jump in. with her
eyes as innocent as a child looking for
love in things it doesn't quite understand
yet. with her smile piecing together the
fragments of my own like a rugged and
rusted fridge. with her hands open and
arms wide, she's looking for a hug she
can stretch around and finally become
someone needed, not just wanted.
with a body exploding with truth,
my meaning in life is to learn the
language of which it speaks. i am
captivated by her and how she
has given hope to someone who once
drowned in a bathtub full of shame
and misery.
we didn't know it then, but wounded
hearts eventually find each other.

she took a picture of herself today.
it was in the morning, before the
world had a chance to touch her.
before the sun was able to speak
of her name. before the moon
drifted off without a goodbye.
before her mouth could utter
a single word and her eyes had
the ability to witness the evil they
normally see. she took a picture
of who she wants to be every day.
not necessarily alone, but if it takes
being that in order to discover the
love and affection needed, then so
be it. there is great value in finding
a reflection you admire and adore.
for some, it comes too late in life
and others they never discover it all.
she's not content, because she knows
the evolution of a soul never ceases.
but the image is wiped clean of the
smudges left when she was incapable
of seeing past her own beauty others
said was never there.

every time i'm with her,
close enough doesn't exist.
as she smiled into my chest,
i took my hand and placed it
under her chin, gently lifting
it, like mountains raising a
wish. in the stillness of our
hearts, i needed the eyes of
my lover to feel the words that
came next, "i don't know how
long i've been without you and
how long it will be until we are
together if it all in this life, but i
will love you feverishly and with
purpose, until we breathe in our
final star."

don't lose your wild
for someone else's dream.

all it took was your
smile for me to know
i am exactly where i
need to be.

i swear that smile of
yours has put me back
together better now than
i ever thought i was before.

maybe her whole life has been made up of men who have said they would, and then walked out when they couldn't handle being one. for those who think she is too much of something else, she never told you she wasn't. you knew and yet you lied to her over and over again. be the man who stays and helps her through these struggles instead of the one who walks away from it. don't be a reason for her to act scared when all she's doing is being herself.

she has fought and died a few times
for the chance at love. every battle
tests the limits of one's character
and forces those limitations to be
written on another breath. her soul
is tired from all of the shattered
promises. her heart is disgusted
by how things have turned out
when she's been putting everything
into them. she's not only defeated
her demons, but also danced with
her guardian angels, and drank the
wine they brought. there's nothing
more glorious than seeing a woman
who is happy about accomplishing
her dreams and the plans she is
making to better her situation.
she enjoys staying up with the moon
to talk to until her heart is no longer
heavy. at the end of the day, it's all in
the glass and going down smoothly;

just like pain subsiding when someone
understands your tears.

don't just be alive.
be a life that helps
someone see hope
in themselves.
never underestimate
your superpower.

do not let anyone tell you that you don't have a good life. you get to play with the sun, moon, and an infinite amount of stars whenever you want to. we decide what's good, and to me, there's nothing better than looking at them with you.

when love finds you,
i hope you consume
all of what you deserve.

and in return,
i can only hope
for you it returns
the favor.

she escaped the mundane
and became reinvigorated
with soul.

it's remarkable what can
happen once you stop
allowing outsiders to
influence your inside
movements.

if my hand ever reaches out
for yours when we are walking
down the street, riding in the car,
or when my anxiety gets the best
of me, hold on please. i get nervous
around crowds and places with a lot
of traffic.

i am a mess that doesn't
need cleaning up, just loved.

the shine is never
gone from your soul.

you just need someone
who knows what they are
looking for when the stars
are no longer in the sky.

she asked me,
"where do you see yourself in five years?"

it was a question i had heard before
multiple times, but somehow
this felt different. an uncontrollable
sensation rolled over my soul as if the
moon directed every wave to hit me at
once. it was the most beautiful
expression and i felt the earth move from
underneath me as i opened my mouth to
try and respond.

"i honestly do not know where i will be
in five, ten, or even forty years, but i know
where the heart of me will be. after this
moment, it will be with you forever and
always, in all ways, with love until the last
beat is given to you."

today, she's celebrating her
independence day. today, she
became brave when all the lights
went out and her soul bursted into
the colors she had dreamt about all
her life.

nothing comes easy when your decision
to let go means venturing out on your
own, but freedom was calling her name
and she was determined to stretch her
bones there. with a mind ready for change,
a heart craving to feel something for the
first time, and her eyes set on finally
being happy, nothing was going to deny
her from discovering true happiness.

there are moments i feel you and
countless hours when i ache just
to hear the sound of your voice.
nothing more is needed to know
you love someone than to know
how incredibly powerful a message
is, right after you get through talking
with them on the phone.
between those two conversations is when
i miss you the most. it's never happened
to me before, but i know the next time
never comes fast enough. all i want to do
is hear how your day went and if it didn't,
my hopes are that i can help you make it
better.
i hear textures in your voice which puts
me at ease and calms all of the anxiety
living inside of me. whatever happens
between you and i, at least i know what
it's like to breathe without the fire
burning me.

wild women live and love between the sun and moon. they dance freely from one adventure to the next. each one is different, but they all share a common bond; they give no explanation for their rebel ways, when they are more than what you expected.

caution signs and flashing lights are not included when you think you are ready for someone like her. you're either all in and skinny dipping with only your soul to show, or you're going to drown in her depths. chances are she will intimidate you, because there's no taming a full moon at the peak of her powers.

she began each
day with a deep
breath and a smile.

but don't be fooled,
even princesses can
become warriors when
tested by dragons.

she is love, and it's just

enough madness to keep

her free from the gravity

surrounding her fears.

she's a fearless ballerina.

the kind that never stops spinning
because the music keeps playing
around her.

the kind that keeps loving no matter
how many sad songs she hears.

the kind that goes on despite the
aches and pains she endures.

keep dancing to everything that makes
you feel beautiful, sweet one, and you will
always have the clouds beneath your feet.

silence
is
a conversation
only
those who have
lived
it can understand.

you frighten people, because you
are in fact whole without needing
anyone else. living in a world where
humans are frantically searching for
a fix, or a long-term solution, you walk
amongst the flowers not competing to be
seen or heard. the act alone is beyond
brave and you're always in full bloom
despite the seasons of change others go
through. there's a reason you smile when
someone says not to, and i hope you
never lose that edge. don't go though life
and allow it to view you as anything other
than the transcendent woman you are.

i am my own
way and i will
forge my path
without consuming
a drop of doubt.

i am in constant search
of self, without imitation.

she wasn't interested in the whole world,
just the whole truth. it's taken her a few
lifetimes to get to this place where she
finally trusts herself. don't kill off another
soul because you can. open yourself up
like a flower looking up for the sun.
be vulnerable, and i promise you'll be
better for it. the ending will always
be finite, but what happens between
each breath creates a reason for you to
keep fighting, or a reason to walk away.
it all comes down to one simple thing:
is it worth your best effort.
if it's not, please leave before you ruin
another butterfly by your touch. we are
all fragile, no matter how much we think
we are invincible. each one of us has the
capability of being the thunder, or the
rain. choose carefully when love is what
you're after.

i saw children crying today with their
hands holding faces i didn't recognize.
i thought to myself, "they are too young
to know this kind of pain." but then again,
what do you expect when every morning
you turn on your tv, there's another
senseless murder or an explosion killing
another dozen or so. i've always wondered
what it would be like if i had kids.
how would i raise them under these
circumstances when people are getting
shot because their color of skin, or being
at the wrong place at the wrong time.
there's nothing logical behind any of it,
just as it doesn't make sense to see kids
crying and consoling adults, telling them,
"it will be okay. the world has been crying
for a long time now. we are just now
seeing the pain come out of the cracks."

i look at them as if they were my own.
i look at them with all the love i have
for my own family as weird as that
sounds, but that's what i do. i love for
the sake of completing what cries out
inside of me. as they took their hands
away from their faces, i saw hope.
their light is too strong to be cast out
by the darkness around them.
they might not have changed the world
right then, but they will one day. as they
walked away from me, flowers began to
rise where they were seated. all it takes is
a little love for life to grow where people
tell you it can't.

she's at a stage in her life where books
save her and people are just reminders
to keep reading. if it doesn't massage
the soul, she knows not to hold onto it
anymore. humans cause the worst kind
of hangovers when you take in too much
of the wrong ones.
life is about moderation, except when it
comes to the beach, wine, good music,
and time spent with those who make you
feel something besides guilty for having
fun. it can become a lonely world for
some, but i promise you, if you stay away
long enough, you'll learn to appreciate
where you end up in your solitude.
trust the vibrations in your bones and
when you're thirsty for adventure, drink
them in entirely as they wash over you.
she's good at making new friends, but
now she knows how to give away her
time to those who make it for her.
she's free falling peacefully back into a
depth that once made her afraid to swim.

now you can't get her out of the water.

she wasn't scared of failing,
because the fear only drove
her wings to grow stronger.

hold her to the flames
and she'll burn down
everything you ever
thought you had.

love is the teacher for
the universe inside of
us.

no matter where we plant
our souls, we will always
grow towards the sun and
moon in our hearts.

we are fragile porcelain
monuments in the eyes
of the stars and must learn
from one another that the
number of times we break
for something or someone
does not dictate who we are.

it only strengthens our will
to become whole once again.

even when i feel nothing, i feel everything at once. it's how i have been my entire life. many would say it's a curse, but i'd rather have it than be numb to the world around me. you'd be surprised by how much grief the bones of the world can carry. for some reason i was made with parts from all the lonely, hoping someone cares about them as much as you say you care about the people you love.

maybe i was born to be alone
forever. days turn to nights
and the sun holds the moon
for as long as it can before
breaking into tears.

when i look up and see two
beings who belong together,
but can't be, it makes sense
why i am here and you are
there.

maybe one day there'll be a
sky that's right for all who
are separated by timing.

she never dreamed about her wedding
or thought about the times she might
be alone after it. time was something
she had lots of, but not always the right
kind. she wanted to dance in the kitchen,
not around lies. she wanted to be pressed
against a wall, not into a corner.
she wanted to be looked at as if she was
the reason you chose her, and not because
you settled for her.
she wanted to be held so tightly,
letting go of her, you yourself would
fall apart. there have been times when
she has doubted everything she has
become, but seeing what could've been,
she can sleep at least knowing she tried.
she never dreamed of a wedding, but she
has seen the future she once saw as a child.
a future as glorious as the first time she
tasted the salt water and fell in love with
how the waves never gave up in their
quest to reach the shore.

one day i'd like to take a walk with you
to some random place and have the most
random conversations and have a glass of
wine with you as i tell you how much i
honestly love you without fear of knowing
why, or how we are where we are.

if it doesn't work out then maybe you
would settle for just a walk as we talk
about how the universe gave us tonight
and how thankful i am for this moment
of certain uncertainty.

there's a possibility she is crazy,
but don't you dare try and change
her. the most glorious things are
and it makes everything else that
much more interesting. we all hope
to find someone like her. someone with
a deadly combination of intelligence and
beauty. someone who will stay up with
you and have those 2am conversations
about taking over the world. where you
find yourself fighting off sleep to keep
your eyes on her a little longer.
someone who finds humor in the most
inappropriate situations and you laugh
because you found someone who gets you.
she isn't a wolf, or a lion. she is the rarest
breed of unicorn who will go to the edge
of the moon and hang her feet just before
she jumps. if you want to do anything in
life worth a damn, jump with her.

she turned her tragedies
into pearls and wore them
without shame.
in life and chance, she bet it
all on her heart without second
guessing her strategy.
her attitude was living until the
final breath was called upon for
one last adventure; something she
would not come back from.
when you aren't afraid of failing,
falling becomes flying without
hesitating. brave, and born with grit,
she became a thousand diamonds
shining without regret. it was never a
job to play wild amongst the ordinary.
she was born to keep life faded off of
her energy.

you are the perfect kind of storm.

the kind that slowly approaches,

building up enough strength to

be heard and the right amount

of vulnerability to be felt.

there are days where i open
a book and just leave it outside
next to me so it can breathe.

with anything delicate and living,
you must.

always live in the
wildness of your heart.
always dance and thrive
where love resides.
always seek out everything
that stirs the depths of the
oceans in you.

waves are created by constant chaos,
and you are forever flowing.
never apologize to others for drowning
in yourself, when you had been searching
for calmer waters, thinking you needed to
be saved.

he took her hand and all at once
she began to cry the tears she kept
behind the dam built by her pain.

he said, "show me the pieces you've
kept hidden, afraid someone could
stop loving you because of them."

she could barely get the word out
of her mouth, but after a few minutes
she asked, "why?"

he brought her into his heart and said,
"i want to see how often you needed me
and i wasn't there to tell you how infinite
you are. if i have the honor of loving just
one of them, i can die knowing i loved the
most beautiful and complete human i've
ever known."

when you find yourself in the dark,
i will not leave your side. when you
feel it coming on, i will be the breath
you need to help your lungs find the
light. one day it will get better and if
it's not today, tomorrow holds a promise
and i will be here with you. when you
have to curl up and put a pillow between
your legs, i'll hold your hand and be right
next to you. i know you don't like to be
held when it happens, but i won't leave
you to fight it alone. we've become a
reflection. we've overcome the distance
that once separated the earth breathing
between us. i am here with you, and as
much as you think i have made you
stronger, i never thought i could carry
two hearts again. some humans are
careless with items labeled fragile when
it's not theirs. i have trust issues and the
times mine had been dropped, it took me
years to find the final pieces. then the
universe found us on a path and decided
we should meet. you've become my
serendipity, and because of that, i am
brave with our love.

i can't pull you closer than this and i guess
this is who we are right now. i can't kiss
you behind the secrets we share and i
guess this is who we are right now.
i can't tell you i love you face to face,
because if i did i wouldn't be able to
leave you. i can't show you the flowers
i have bought and the notes i wrote to
go with them. i can't hold you any tighter
than this and i guess this is who we are
right now. there's a lot of guessing going
into this, because what we are trying to do
isn't how a relationship works.
i've learned how to love a soul and not a
body. i've learned how to kiss a dream and
say goodnight in the same breath. and the
sad part is, i'm not sure we will ever be
more than this. i will divulge a secret and
not ask one from you in return. if this is
all we become, you will always be the
name i call out when i need saving.
you will always be the lyrics to every song
i hear and the wind brushing up against
me when i feel alone. you will always be
the reason i believed in myself again,
and because of you, i am able to see you
down the road. even if the road leads to
nowhere, i'd rather be traveling towards
it, because i know i won't be alone.

i want to be strong for you and show
you i don't flinch at the first sound of
something going wrong. i want to be
able to hold you tight enough that you
knew if i ever let go, my arms would fall
at my side and never move the same again.
i want to make promises i know would
never be broken, and if they did,
you would understand and i wouldn't
hang my head in shame. i want to watch
you walk down the aisle of sand, while my
heart makes it hard for me to keep still.
i want to take your hand and not just give
you a ring, but a kind of love of which will
never leave you. i want to kiss you and
seal the fate of every star we ever wished
upon in hopes of finding each other
without knowing for certain we ever
would. i want to read you poems i wrote
on your soul long before we spoke a single
word. i want us, and however it works out,
what you've granted me is a lasting
memory i will always go back to watch.
it's where happiness found a man once
removed from death, and barely hanging
onto a bottle he thought would save him.

i guess i am a jealous person.

it's funny because i've never been my
entire life until i met you. there are
times when i am jealous of the fact
we don't have memories to speak of
and everyone else who has loved you,
they do. knowing they've had their
moments with you while i cannot is
maddening. i've had this saying in my
head for months, "patience of the heart
tells a lot about the soul of a person."
i would like to think i am patient,
considering all of the things i have been
through and all of the things i am still
wishing to do one day. always know that
my heart is growing with each breath the
universe takes, in hopes of sharing my
love with you until the sun finally fades
from our view. i guess i am jealous,
but it's only because i love you more
than anybody else ever will.

your eyes make me wonder how a woman
can hold so much pain and love inside of
them at the same time. your smile makes
me wonder how many times you've truly
made miracles happen by using it the way
you do. your face makes me wonder how
many times people have seen the same
thing i have, and blinked as they said
goodbye. your heart makes me believe
that art doesn't have to be seen to be
appreciated. your voice makes me
understand how the sun feels when the
moon whispers to it when they are given
enough time to be themselves.
you intrigue me in so many ways
and i can only hope one day i'll know
how it feels to lie next to you, with my
hand in yours. only then will i fully
understand why the spaces between
my fingers never fit with anyone else.

stand tall, sweet one.
you are far too beautiful
to hang your head over
someone who never
bothered looking up to
see what he had.
don't become blind to what
others never saw.
you've got a smile that can
change the way a star is made.
keep your shoulders free of the
guilt put on by those who were
too weak to carry their own.

there's a lot of love out there to take
in, and it's waiting on you without
judgment.

she loved to swim,
but always drowned
herself for others
who never made the
same effort to meet
her past the depths
of her own heart.

transitioning from one self to another
is the most difficult thing we as humans
will ever do. it's during each phase we
find parts of ourselves we love and hate
equally. the struggle comes when you love
someone who stays the same throughout
the relationship. if neither of you are
growing, the bond you thought you
shared will be forever lost.

you will need to move on from this type
of love and find someone who will help
you and encourage you through the
change, as well as their own.

one of the hardest parts of life is loving
someone who is already holding a heart
of which doesn't belong to you.

deep down you know this person is
meant to be more involved in your life,
and it's about deciding when holding
them there becomes too much of a
burden for you to carry any further.
sometimes we don't get what we think
we need, but we will always receive just
enough to keep going until we are where
we should be. choices make or break us
and form our soul's structure.

if you're in the midst of making one,
break for something with the power
to destroy you. only then will you
appreciate what you have.

there she goes again, being beautiful,
as if the universe itself gave birth to
her smile.
heartache and pain fall from her wings
like memories cascading down the earth's
face.
there she goes again, laughing, as if the
problems she faced didn't exist and the
humans around her actually loved each
other equally.
you could say this world wasn't meant for
her, but the sun and moon both love her
too much to stay down for long.
there comes a time in life when you start
seeing things through the eyes of the
child you once were. where you start
believing in the fairy-tales again.
where you begin to love the skin you've
been given to walk around in until your
soul is ready to fly. she's living proof
everything exists, and it if it doesn't,
it once did. her crown still shines,
even with the dents and scratches it
has accumulated.

i love who i am with you.
it's been such a journey
discovering what moves
me and who stood by me
when heaven was too busy
taking names to notice mine.
i believe in things others never
will and i couldn't be any happier
with it. cast me out as an outsider
if you must, but i will not build walls,
only roads for those who wish to
visit me. the most important thing
in life is keeping an open mind as
well as looking out of the third eye
others declare is blind and non-existent.
i'm finally content with my beliefs, but i
will feverishly pursue the other side of
perfection. i have no idea what the
absolute definition of life is, but loving
you brings me closer with each picture
i take of you with my heart.

it's an unfinished album with empty
pages containing the moments i am
looking forward to the most.

she will make you do incredible
things and make you believe in
the most beautiful ways to breathe.
she once walked barefoot on the
moon just to prove to herself she
could. she's been dreaming for years
about getting out of the small town
that's been holding her down for quite
some time now. her hope has been
blinded by men telling her one thing
and then each giving examples of why
she stopped trusting a long time ago.
it's only a matter of time before the
road starts moving again, but until
then, she's planting the seeds needed
to replace the flowers life had stolen
from her last year. you may be able
to take a few things from her, but she
knows how to salvage the remains in
order to create a meaningful life
without you.

i am caught between the
moon and sun again.

where feelings are disguised
as stars, and you are hoping
to find one that will fall for
your faults.

she's wanted and wild, with a heart gone
mad for love. they say too much of a good
thing can kill you, but it only makes her
fly higher. there's no sense in trying to
understand her next move, just let her
roam free with the brave ones who don't
believe in limits. she's that broken smile
you've heard about, who points to the lost
and calls them home.

it just made sense to love you like this.
not everyone creates a smile like this
and not everyone is strong enough to
keep it when the world does everything
it can to bury you beneath the layers of
its skin. it just made sense to love you like
this. it's not every day you get to wake up
to someone who takes your covers and
wish they'd take them all if it meant they
are at peace. it's not every day you get to
close your eyes with someone to only
meet them again in your favorite place
within minutes of kissing her portrait of
a soul. like this is what tomorrow will be
and like this is what makes right now
worth the time you missed out on
in-between the breaths you took without
them.

she is a world

the stars walked

into and a universe

the world will never forget.

we are the sleepless dreamers, with a
fire made from passion. we are the
thirsty flowers reaching for sunlight.
we are the footprints left on the universe
after everything else has left this life.
we are the echoes of the canyons rebelling
against the borders that try and keep us
cornered. we are both the eye and
madness of the storms passing through
those who think they are somehow better
than you and i. we are the writings on
every wall that has been built in order to
create a life where art is forever lasting.
we wear our skin at times colored in
camouflage, hoping no one sees us,
so we can be left alone from all the evil
hiding amongst us. inside of me are
devils, angels, and monsters all fighting
for a place at the table. we are what we see,
and what i see is a man still accepting his
failures and misfortunes. what i see is not
a mistake. what i see is misunderstood
love and misplaced anger for those who
left me. i am an unfinished product in a
factory making promises to all of us.
i am delicate and unpolished.
i am not human...

i have too much soul to wear that label.

she cried so hard she gave
herself a headache. the kind
you hope runs back to wherever
it came from because you cannot
sleep it away.
she's an emotional reader and invests
her energy into each one she opens.
her gentle spirit has been known to
laugh out loud or question them,
but that's who she is in life. she doesn't
hide behind the pages like most.
when she was little, after everyone had
gone to bed, she'd sneak a flashlight into
her room and finish whatever she was
reading. in her head, she gives herself a
cutoff point, but we all know once you're
in a book you can't put down,
time becomes an imaginary world where
anything can happen.

brave girl,

> you were made for far more
> beautiful things. chaos is only
> understood when it is loved by
> the wild, not the weak.

it wasn't magic and it didn't happen
overnight. it took years for her to see
the value in things. it took a lifetime
to understand not everyone you meet
is meant to serve you the same as you
do yourself.
value silence when everyone else is
talking. those moments define the soul
of a person and it's only then can you
hear their true thoughts.
maybe it was her way of connecting to
each star she touched and every galaxy
she held, trying to become something
she wasn't. she's at a different point of
direction now, and before when she
turned east, she now goes west just to
get away from the noise. it's a path she
cut out by using the pieces others had
broken off. but she's growing back what
was once lost, one punch at a time. a true
beauty in her entirety, she's a goddess at
this moment, taking in all the thunder
and lightning that comes her way.
life will eventually attempt to drag her
down again, though this time she's held
onto the darkness that almost killed her
as a remembrance of what she can do,
once you've survived the heart of hell.

when you love her,

don't take it for granted.

there's a reason why she has

entrusted you with her vibe.

keep earning it for as long as

you are able to breathe in her

colors.

he may have loved you, but i will mean
it when i am still standing beside you
after our first argument.

long after our first dance, our hearts will
still be one beating soul. the constellation
that tied us together and created our
story will continue to grow with each
step we take.

as we look up and count the stars,
let's not forget the ones we are holding.

we have always been different in the
sense of believing in things others find
silly. i beg you, never stop being silly with
me, lover.

when you make love to her,
always look her in the soul.
when you are ascending in
love, be there in your entirety.
she deserves the very best from
you. it shouldn't take her asking
for it in order for you to show it.

magic demands to be
felt, not wished for.

your eyes are a living
mystery, with a million
wishes living within the
edges of your being.

your hair is comprised
of disregard and amnesia.

your face is pure existence
of love which i find myself
a believer of.

clarity is marked with empty
boxes, especially when you
have no answer for what
you are seeing.

i am not confused by what is in front of
me.

i am simply trying to figure out how to
open my mouth to say hello.

reassure her about your love when you
can. even if she believes you the first
time, she'll always love hearing it.
don't leave her in the morning without
painting her body with meaningful kisses
all over the places you missed the night
before. when you tell her you longed for
her during the day, put both of your
hands on her face, look her in the eyes,
take a deep breath, and exhale everything
you feel for her. give her the little things
as often as you can. leave her messages
that will make her laugh and giggle even
when she's with company. she's never
playing hard to get. she just wants to see
how far you will go for her. she may be the
type to go silent from time to time, and
it's

during those moments you will need to hold her the closest. the walls she built before you might go up every now and again, but don't be afraid to climb them to get to her. she will survive long after you if your decision is to leave. all she needs is for you to be honest about why you love her, and if you're ever unhappy, speak your mind. there are too many of us walking around, talking to others about why it didn't work out. the world is full of psychiatrists after the fact. especially when all it took was a little more effort and understanding.

never beg anyone to be their
first choice when you are not
even your own. life is full of
what ifs, but losing sleep,
thinking about if they care
for you the same shouldn't be
a reason you stay to figure out
if it can work. what matters most
is remembering to love yourself
when you said you would.

broken promises will happen, but to
continually go out of your way for
another who doesn't consider who you
are to be engaging or unforgettable,
remove your light from their darkness.
one day you'll meet someone who you
can find love in the shadows with,
without using all of your energy to create
a source of power.

life is way too short to blind yourself for
others who are colorblind to your colors.

she's the type of woman who looks sexy even in a bad mood. you can't help but try your best to make her smile. out of all the faces you will encounter over the course of your life, it is in the raging sea of faces you will look for hers. in the confines of a mystery, she is the type to give you truth, as you look for the next move at solving yourself. she doesn't cross words or feelings, and it's because of this reason you will be surrendering your heart by the end of the day. whether she takes it or leaves you bleeding in your own pool of misfortunes, you're going to die trying for her hand. she's the type of woman who doesn't need you, but you will always be tirelessly searching for her. a limited edition of all things mystical, she's a rarity that only comes around once in a blue moon. and here you are, holding your breath, hoping to change the color of the night.